362.299
R576s

MAY
2009

Steroids

David Robson

Drugs

ReferencePoint
Press™

San Diego, CA

© 2009 ReferencePoint Press, Inc.

For more information, contact:
ReferencePoint Press, Inc.
PO Box 27779
San Diego, CA 92198
www. ReferencePointPress.com

Picture credits:
Maury Aaseng: 30–32, 46–48, 61–63, 73–76
AP Images: 11, 14

LIBRARY OF CONGRESS CATALOGING-IN-PUBLICATION DATA

Robson, David, 1966–
  Steroids / by David Robson.
    p. cm. — (Compact research)
  Includes bibliographical references and index.
  ISBN-13: 978-1-60152-067-8 (hardback)
  ISBN-10: 1-60152-067-0 (hardback)
  1. Steroid abuse. 2. Anabolic steroids—Health aspects. 3. Doping in sports. I. Title.
  HV5822.S68.R63 2008
  362.29'9—dc22

                                               2008039766

Contents

Foreword

As modern civilization continues to evolve, its ability to create, store, distribute, and access information expands exponentially. The explosion of information from all media continues to increase at a phenomenal rate. By 2020 some experts predict the worldwide information base will double every 73 days. While access to diverse sources of information and perspectives is paramount to any democratic society, information alone cannot help people gain knowledge and understanding. Information must be organized and presented clearly and succinctly in order to be understood. The challenge in the digital age becomes not the creation of information, but how best to sort, organize, enhance, and present information.

ReferencePoint Press developed the *Compact Research* series with this challenge of the information age in mind. More than any other subject area today, researching current issues can yield vast, diverse, and unqualified information that can be intimidating and overwhelming for even the most advanced and motivated researcher. The *Compact Research* series offers a compact, relevant, intelligent, and conveniently organized collection of information covering a variety of current topics ranging from illegal immigration and methamphetamine to diseases such as anorexia and meningitis.

The series focuses on three types of information: objective single-author narratives, opinion-based primary source quotations, and facts and statistics. The clearly written objective narratives provide context and reliable background information. Primary source quotes are carefully selected and cited, exposing the reader to differing points of view. And facts and statistics sections aid the reader in evaluating perspectives. Presenting these key types of information creates a richer, more balanced learning experience.

For better understanding and convenience, the series enhances information by organizing it into narrower topics and adding design features that make it easy for a reader to identify desired content. For example, in *Compact Research: Illegal Immigration*, a chapter covering the economic impact of illegal immigration has an objective narrative explaining the various ways the economy is impacted, a balanced section of numerous primary source quotes on the topic, followed by facts and full-color illustrations to encourage evaluation of contrasting perspectives.

The ancient Roman philosopher Lucius Annaeus Seneca wrote, "It is quality rather than quantity that matters." More than just a collection of content, the *Compact Research* series is simply committed to creating, finding, organizing, and presenting the most relevant and appropriate amount of information on a current topic in a user-friendly style that invites, intrigues, and fosters understanding.

Steroids at a Glance

Prevalence

Americans have been warned for years about the risks of steroid use, yet studies show more people—athletes and nonathletes—are using steroids now than ever before.

Body Image

Young people, especially young men, are turning to steroids in the hope of developing the media-driven "ideal" body type as well as improving their athletic capabilities.

Health Risks

Although prolonged steroid use damages a user's health and well-being, steroids are still widely used by athletes in many sports such as cycling, baseball, and track and field.

Professional Sports

Until recently, many professional sports organizations have paid little attention to the spread of steroid use. Sports such as hockey, golf, and baseball are still grappling with how to deal with the problem.

High School and College Athletes

Over the past decade testing for steroids and punishing those found to be using them has become a priority of officials in high school and college programs.

Laws

In recent years the U.S. federal government has held numerous hearings and passed a variety of laws to call attention to the problem of steroids and to penalize those willing to sell or use them.

Prevention

Many experts are now calling for early education programs to inform young people about the health risks and the ethical implications of using performance-enhancing drugs such as steroids.

Overview

66 The use of performance-enhancing drugs like steroids in baseball, football and other sports is dangerous. It sends the wrong message that there are shortcuts to accomplishment and that performance is more important than character. . . . I call on team owners, union representatives, coaches and players to take the lead, to send the right signal, to get tough and to get rid of steroids now.99

—George W. Bush, 2004 State of the Union Address.

66 Doctors ought to quit worrying about what ballplayers are taking. What players take doesn't matter. It's nobody else's business. The doctors should spend their time looking for cures for cancer.99

—Baseball player Barry Bonds, comment to the Associated Press.

Anabolic steroids, often referred to simply as steroids, are drugs used for both legitimate medical purposes and to enhance an athlete's physical size, strength, and speed. Those most prone to nonmedical steroid use are weight lifters and bodybuilders, for whom well-defined muscles or enormous power are a requirement of their sport. Yet during the last two decades, other athletes have stoked controversy by their alleged steroid use. Former professional baseball star José Canseco made headlines in 2005 when he admitted to taking the banned drugs during his career as well as injecting some of his teammates. But Canseco, in his book *Juiced*, offered no apologies. Indeed, he bragged about the effects steroids had on his body: "Certain steroids, used in proper combinations, can cure certain diseases. Steroids will give you a better quality of life and also drastically slow down the aging process. I'm forty years old, but I look much younger."[1]

While Canseco's conclusions about steroids are medically unsound, he is not alone in his belief that they can be beneficial, especially in enhancing athletic performance. Tufts University physicist Roger Tobin studied the effects of steroids in professional baseball and found that a 10 percent increase in muscle mass makes a stark difference when swinging a bat: "A 4 percent increase in [batted] ball speed, which can reasonably be expected from steroid use, can increase home run production by anywhere from 50 percent to 100 percent."[2]

Yet a majority of health professionals warn of the potential side effects and long-term dangers, many of which are only now being discovered. Among these in men are acne, baldness, testicle shrinkage, reduced sperm count, infertility, breast development, and heart and liver disease. In women, side effects may include acne, facial hair, baldness, deepened voice, clitoral enlargement, and erratic menstrual cycle.

The physical dangers are just one of the concerns associated with steroids. Another important consideration is whether enhancing one's performance by taking illegal drugs constitutes cheating. Should a sprinter who has increased her muscle mass and strength by taking steroids be allowed to compete against a person who has not? Is a gold medal won by a "juiced" swimmer as legitimate as the medal earned by the athlete who has not taken performance-enhancing drugs? And what kind of message do steroid users send to young people? For Linn Goldberg, specialist in sports medicine and an expert on the use of steroids in sports, this question is paramount: "My greater concern is not about professional athletics, but how those athletes who cheat and tarnish sports impact children and adolescents."[3]

> **Former professional baseball star José Canseco made headlines in 2005 when he admitted to taking the banned drugs during his career as well as injecting some of his teammates.**

Pumping Iron

Anabolic steroids are known by many nicknames: juice, sauce, slop, and roids, among them. Users take the drugs either by injecting them directly into their muscles or by rubbing the cream or gel form into their skin. Often they are taken in combination with other performance-enhancing drugs or other steroids. This practice is known as "stacking." The user takes them over a certain period of time, or "cycle," to achieve the desired effect.

Steroids helped Craig Costa, a former high school athlete, get "insanely big—like an action figure."[4] He loved flexing his muscles in front of the mirror and eventually grew his 5'9" frame to 225 pounds (102kg). But over time Costa's appearance and health took a turn for the worse. His face became puffy; red, blotchy acne exploded across his back; and his thick hair fell out in clumps. Then the chest pains began. By now Costa had a son and wanted to live long enough to see him grow up. He stopped taking steroids cold turkey. Although Craig Costa survived his steroids ordeal, a recent investigative report in the *Dallas Morning News* suggests that he is not alone in his attraction to these illegal drugs. In some Texas school districts, 8 percent of student athletes take steroids. And while statistics vary from state to state, the true measure of the problem may be impossible to gauge. Users are reluctant to come clean about their habit.

> " Anabolic steroids are known by many nicknames: juice, sauce, slop, and roids, among them. "

Greg Schwab, a football, wrestling, and track coach, sees this desire in young people for extreme size as a symptom of a larger problem: "They're being raised with this incredibly competitive attitude. It used to be that we played sports for the camaraderie experience, for the team, for the fun of it. Now kids play competitive sports because it's a means to an end. It's a way to get a scholarship."[5]

This fierce sense of competition has encouraged individual athletes to consider the drugs a necessity. American track star Marion Jones did. The statuesque athlete trained for years in anticipation of winning gold in the 100-meter race and the long jump. Her hard work paid off when Jones

These steroids were confiscated by the DEA in an 18-month international investigation of illegal steroid labs. In recent years the U.S. government has held numerous hearings and passed a variety of laws to call attention to the problem of steroids and to penalize those willing to sell or use them.

won 3 gold medals and two bronze at the 2000 Olympic Games in Sydney, Australia. She returned home a hero and reaped millions of dollars in product endorsement deals. But in 2004 the International Olympic Committee opened an investigation into Jones's rumored steroid use. Jones denied using steroids but suspicion increased when she tested positive for erythropoietin (EPO), often referred to as the "endurance athlete's steroid," in 2006. Before long, the pressure and accusations forced her confession.

In October 2007 Jones wrote a letter to family and friends in which she admitted using a hard-to-detect steroid called "the clear" before the Sydney games. Soon after, she publicly admitted her drug use. The medals Jones won were revoked, and Jones spent six months in jail for previously lying to federal agents. "It's the destruction of a heroine of the day," said Dick Pound, chairman of the World Anti-Doping Agency. "It's sad at one level, but it's still tawdry cheating at another level."[6]

The Origins of Steroids

The history of anabolic steroids goes back 120 years. In 1889 neurologist Charles-Édouard Brown-Séquard, who had previously done pioneering work on blood and the nervous system, developed the idea that the human body contains substances now known as hormones. These substances, Brown-Séquard hypothesized, affect the organs in the body. In his later years he experimented on dogs and guinea pigs, eventually extracting fluid from their testicles and injecting himself with it. The injections, he claimed, prolonged a person's life. Although Brown-Séquard lived to be 77 years old—a ripe old age at the time—how responsible the canines and rodents were for his longevity remains unclear.

> While statistics vary from state to state, the true measure of the problem may be impossible to gauge. Users are reluctant to come clean about their habit.

But Brown-Séquard was on to something. Testosterone was isolated in the laboratory by scientists in 1935 and named by combining the words *testicle* and the suffix of *ketone,* which is a chemical compound. Soon after, chemists created a synthetic—or human-made—version of the real thing. These anabolic steroids are similar in type to the male hormone testosterone. The term "anabolic" refers to the drug's ability to enhance cell growth.

The earliest known reference to anabolic steroids as muscle-building agents dates to a 1938 letter to the editor in *Strength and Health* magazine. During World War II, German scientists injected concentration camp victims with steroids in an effort to keep them from wasting away due to lack of food. Some Nazis soldiers also received injections in an attempt to make them more aggressive.

Not until the 1960s did athletes begin using anabolic steroids as a way of enhancing their athletic performance. Although few professional athletes today will admit to using them, alleged users, including baseball phenomenon Barry Bonds, have seen their statistics on the field skyrocket. Bonds, for example, saw his at-bats per home run numbers go from 9.8 in 2000 to 6.5 in 2001. In other words, he needed approximately 3 fewer swings at the ball to knock it out of the park. Researchers John McCloskey and Julian Bailes are convinced that "the use of performance-enhancing drugs is the only thing capable of boosting that figure."[7]

Steroids and Medicine

Media attention remains focused on the controversy surrounding steroids in sports, but steroids have been used for decades to treat the symptoms of deadly diseases such as cancer and acquired immunodeficiency syndrome, or AIDS. Certain steroids, including dexamethasone and prednisolone, help reduce swelling in cancer patients. They have also been found to help alleviate nausea associated with chemotherapy. One useful side effect of taking steroids during cancer treatment is increased appetite. Cortisone, another commonly used steroid, is used to treat skin irritations, allergies, asthma, arthritis, and a variety of eye diseases. Another performance-enhancing steroid is erythropoietin, or EPO. The kidneys produce and release this protein. When taken by athletes, EPO helps increase endurance; doctors, meanwhile, use it to treat anemia in their patients.

Whether steroids are taken for purely medicinal purposes or not, they usually affect the body dramatically. According to one 1996 study, "Men who exercised and took steroids for 10 weeks put on an average of 13 pounds of muscle and could bench press an extra 48 pounds."[8] But steroids are not miracle drugs. They build muscle mass and add to an athlete's strength, but they will not transform anyone into a superhero. "It will not turn an average athlete into an elite athlete," says Linn Goldberg. "It will enhance a person's performance depending on the amount they use and the type of training they undergo."[9]

> " This fierce sense of competition has encouraged individual athletes to consider the drugs a necessity. "

How Serious a Problem Is Steroid Use?

The most recent statistics on steroid use suggest that while most young people avoid the temptation to enhance their bodies by taking such drugs, others do indulge themselves. According to recent studies, between late middle school and the last year of high school, roughly 2 percent of students use

Don Hooton, looking at his son's belongings, wonders if he could have prevented his son's death. Taylor Hooton, who was 17, committed suicide when he became depressed after stopping his steroid use.

or have used steroids. While this percentage may seem small, it does mean that hundreds of thousands of adolescents have experimented with steroids. A 2005 investigative story in the *Dallas Morning News* found that in Texas, at least, steroids were making a comeback in high schools, but few people were willing to talk about it: "I've never witnessed a behavior as secretive as this," said steroids researcher Charles Yesalis. "People will tell you they smoked pot, they did coke, they did speed, they did crank, they smacked their wife, they smacked their girlfriend long before they tell you they used anabolic steroids."[10]

For years, the hush-hush use of performance-enhancing drugs such as steroids extended into the world of professional sports as well. Yet all that began to change as witnesses to the doping of professional athletes were pressured to tell what they knew. Former baseball trainer Brian McNamee made headlines in December 2007 when he revealed to federal authorities that seven-time Cy Young Award winner Roger Clemens used steroids. Although rumors of Clemens's steroid use had circulated for years, McNamee confirmed them before the U.S. Congress in early 2008. "During the time that I worked with Roger Clemens I injected him on numerous occasions with steroids and human growth hormone."[11] In a now famous retort on the television news program *60 Minutes*, Clemens adamantly denied McNamee's accusations: "My body never changed," Clemens said. "If he's putting that stuff up in my body, if what he's saying, which is totally false, if he's doing that to me, I should have a third ear coming out of my forehead. I should be pulling tractors with my teeth."[12] Yet Clemens and other star athletes, including cyclist Floyd Landis, guilty or not, have been tainted by accusations that they achieved incredible athletic feats by using steroids. And Landis was stripped of his 2007 Tour de France victory because of it.

> " Clemens and other star athletes, including cyclist Floyd Landis, guilty or not, have been tainted by accusations that they achieved incredible athletic feats by using steroids. "

How Dangerous Are Steroids?

Scientists have determined that the two main effects synthetic testosterone, or steroids, have on the body are androgenic and anabolic. The androgenic outcomes, in both males and females, include growth in body hair, a deepening of the voice, bone growth, and added strength. These androgenic side effects are coupled with the anabolic effects, where muscle tissue growth quickly increases. While beard growth, diminished breast size, and the onset of a baritone voice may discourage steroid use by some females, the supplements tend to reinforce and encourage a sense of extreme "manliness" in their male counterparts.

Yet men are not exempt from the possible side effects of steroids. Certain users have reported a shrinking of their testicles, breast enlargement, and mood swings. Even more alarming for men and women is the potential for high blood pressure and cholesterol levels, liver damage, severe acne, and fluid retention.

Also of concern are the effects of steroids on teen users. Bones continue growing during puberty and even beyond. But one cycle of steroids often stunts, or completely halts, bone development in young people. The side effects suffered by adults—the acne, hair loss, and liver damage—is magnified in teens.

Despite the warnings, others argue that the dangers of steroids are overstated. In short-term users, side effects such as bad skin and shrunken or swollen genitals usually go away once the user stops taking the steroids. And while some studies suggest links between steroids and depression or suicidal feelings, these studies are less than conclusive.

Why Do People Take Steroids?

For enthusiastic steroid takers, any potential physical danger often diminishes and is overshadowed by the stunning results they get from taking the drugs. Pick up any bodybuilding magazine and you will see the stark and often grotesque results that would likely be impossible without the ingestion of massive doses of steroids, steroid alternatives such as human growth hormone (HGH), or other dietary supplements.

> One cycle of steroids often stunts, or completely halts, bone development in young people.

Kelli White made her name not as a bodybuilder but as a track star. She won both the 100- and 200-meter races at the 2003 World Championships and was labeled the fastest woman in the world. But few knew she had been doping as a way of combating injury. Like so many athletes who take steroids, she rationalized her actions. "I felt like, well, everybody else is doing it," she says. But despite the side effects—the deep voice, the irregular menstrual cycle—"it never, ever made me want to stop doing it."[13]

Only after a positive test for the banned stimulant modafinil did White's world begin falling apart. She eventually confessed to using other substances, including the designer steroids THG and EPO. Designer steroids differ on a molecular level from known—and often illegal—steroids. Thus, by slightly changing the chemical makeup of a drug, scientists can help athletes and other users avoid detection. Kelli White's admission resulted in a two-year ban from her sport.

An outright banning from a sport encourages athletes to think twice before indulging in illicit performance enhancers. The allure of fame and fortune, the temptation to trade honesty for multimillion-dollar contracts and extraordinary media attention, is persuasive to many athletes. Others claim they must take the drugs simply to keep up with their competition.

> An outright banning from a sport encourages athletes to think twice before indulging in illicit performance enhancers.

Should Steroid Testing and Laws Be Strengthened?

In December 2007 the Mitchell Report was released. Named for former U.S. senator George Mitchell, who headed the study, the report dropped like a bombshell on the world of professional sports. Confined to baseball, the 409-page document identified 86 names, including 7 Most Valuable Players and 31 All-Stars, as steroid users. "Those who have illegally used these substances range from players whose major league careers were brief to potential members of the Baseball Hall of Fame," Mitchell wrote. "They include both pitchers and position players, and their backgrounds are as diverse as those of all major league players."[14]

Mitchell's work was a clear indictment of baseball's lax attitude toward steroid use among its players. Yet it also suggested the need for tougher laws and testing in professional sports. In the case of Major League Baseball, steroids have been banned since 1991, but testing did not begin until 2003. Initially, only one random test per player was required. In 2005 year-round testing was implemented, and in November of that year a 50-game ban for a first offense and a lifetime ban for a third offense was implemented.

And while steroid use is illegal, private laboratories around the world continue creating substances that provide the potency of testosterone. What makes testing so difficult is that the chemical makeup of substances can be altered slightly so as to be nearly undetectable in drug tests. The hard fact is that athletes who want to "juice" will often find a way to do it, despite the best efforts of athletic officials and politicians.

How Can Steroid Use Be Prevented?

No simple solution to steroid use has been found, but many experts agree that early education can make a difference. Since 2005, the National Federation of State High School Associations has funded the Make the Right Choice campaign, which includes DVDs and other resources to help warn teenagers about the danger of taking steroids.

Other popular programs are ATLAS (Adolescents Training and Learning to Avoid Steroids) and ATHENA (Athletes Targeting Healthy Exercise and Nutrition Alternatives). The programs' goals are to encourage healthy living and reduce the use of steroids and other drugs among high school athletes. Although the programs have been in existence for more than a decade, in 2007 the National Football League became a partner by providing a $1.2 million grant.

> **Mitchell's work was a clear indictment of baseball's lax attitude toward steroid use among its players.**

Like Make the Right Choice, the partnership provides resources and encourages young people to say no to steroids. Demonte Queen, a former squad leader at Fairmont Heights High School outside of Washington, D.C., praised the program: "I don't think steroids were a problem in our school, but (ATLAS) was a good program. I eat better now, and I've stayed away from steroids."[15]

Queen is not unique in choosing to avoid steroids, but the stark truth is that many others will make a different choice. Experts recognize the attraction of steroids: athletes seek a competitive edge; others simply want to look more physically fit. Yet most remain hopeful that education can lessen the temptation and convince young people to lead healthier, drug-free lives.

How Serious a Problem Is Steroid Use?

❝I can't remember even hearing anybody talk about it. You don't want to be naive, but we have our own issues, and steroids is not one of them.❞

—NBA All-Star Grant Hill.

❝Steroid use is a national public health crisis. This legislation is aimed at not only getting rid of performance enhancing drugs on the professional level, but also sends a message loud and clear to the young people of America: Steroids are illegal. Steroids are dangerous. They can be deadly. And there is no place for them in our sports leagues or our school grounds.❞

—U.S. representative Tom Davis, upon introduction of the Clean Sports Act of 2005.

D etermining exactly how many people use anabolic steroids is difficult. Those prone to using drugs to enhance their physiques or athletic performances are unlikely to announce it in press releases. Instead, steroids often exist in a shadowy world where what is seen is left unspoken and what is heard remains little more than hearsay. Then again, the outright pressure to use can be intense.

Patrick, a student in Texas's Colleyville High School, was prodded by friends and coaches to get bigger. Even his dad, a former star athlete in high school, encouraged his son to do whatever it took to improve his strength and speed on the football field. Lifting weights simply would not be enough to achieve the results he (and everyone else) wanted. So, after paying one of the senior boys $200, Patrick received delivery of a small vial of the steroid nandrolone decanoate, or "deca," in the driveway of his home. Then after buying some 22-gauge needles at the local Walgreens, Patrick began injecting himself with the powerful drug.

The pressure Patrick felt was not out of the ordinary, says another former teen user, Cameron: "The kids are always like, 'You need to get bigger because these kids that you're going to play now are going to be huge.' Right now they're saying they don't want to [use steroids]. But when you get on varsity and actually see the real picture of how big these guys are, you never know—they might start."[16]

By the Numbers

An early study of anabolic steroid use in middle and high school indicated a relatively modest number of student users. The 1991 statistics suggested that across the country, 1.9 percent of eighth graders had tried steroids. By 1999 that number had increased to 2.7 percent. Two years later the percentage had settled slightly to 2.5 percent. The rate starkly increased once students reached high school. Only 1.8 percent of tenth graders took steroids in 1991, but that rate increased to 3.5 percent by 2002. Even more twelfth graders had tried the drugs—4 percent by 2002.

> Steroids often exist in a shadowy world where what is seen is left unspoken and what is heard remains little more than hearsay.

In certain parts of the United States, such percentages were low. A 2002 Texas study, for example, reported the use of steroids at double the national average. In one Lone Star State school district, 8 percent of high school seniors said they had used steroids.

Some Texans disputed the findings: "I'm telling you, I've never seen it, and I've never suspected it," said Mike Hughes, football coach and athletic director at Plano West. "I'm more concerned about other things— alcohol, marijuana and those things."[17]

Jack Elam, athletic director and former head football coach at Rockwall High School, found the steroid statistics shocking; like Hughes, he says they did not jibe with his personal experience: "The numbers you're taking off that survey and the actual kids that I coached, they don't go hand in hand."[18]

A more recent study, released in 2007, involved more than 3,200 students in 12 states, including New Jersey, Pennsylvania, and New Mexico. Of students surveyed, 1.6 percent (2.4 percent of boys and 0.8 percent of girls) admitted using anabolic steroids. This percentage is lower than a 2005 national report that suggested 4 percent of kids in grades 9 through 12 took steroids. What accounts for the discrepancy is hard to determine, but author of the study, Jay Hoffman, blames steroid use on 2 factors: a lack of education among young people and professional players who "juice." Hoffman, who also serves as chair of the Department of Health and Exercise Science at the College of New Jersey, feels that pro athletes are failing youth: "I believe there is an inherent responsibility of being a role model. Whether they want it or not, it comes with the territory."[19]

> " Despite regular denials, the statistics . . . paint a troubling portrait of high school and professional sports and anabolic steroid use in general. "

At the professional level few hard numbers back up accusations of steroid taking, although some informal estimates put steroid use among players as high as 80 percent. While such a high rate of steroid use seems unlikely, little doubt remains that the high stakes of professional sports have convinced many of the best athletes in the world to use the drugs. Despite regular denials, the statistics—even if not completely accurate—paint a troubling portrait of high school and professional sports and anabolic steroid use in general.

Who Uses Steroids?

Perhaps surprisingly, the typical consumers of anabolic steroids are not professional, college, or even teen athletes. They are well-educated white men who are not even necessarily athletes. "Basically, in a nutshell," says researcher Jack Darkes of the University of South Florida, "the typical user is a fairly highly educated, gainfully employed Caucasian of about 30 years old, not motivated by sports for the most part."[20]

Instead, the goal for many of these men is muscle mass, added strength, and physical attractiveness. Steroids, these men believe, will keep away their beer bellies and raise their confidence levels in social settings. Rick Collins, coauthor of a 2007 study on the subject, says, "The users we surveyed consider that they are using directed drug technology as one part of a strategy for physical self-improvement within a health-centered lifestyle."[21]

> **Female steroid users are often looking to improve their bodies and their looks, too, but for them the steroid taking may have a unique psychological component.**

Female steroid users are often looking to improve their bodies and their looks, too, but for them the steroid taking may have a unique psychological component. According to the book *It's Not About Food* by eating-disorder experts Carol Emery Normandi and Laurelee Roark, "Each time a woman says 'I feel fat,' she is doing what she has been taught to do: she is making a comment about her body instead of sorting through the conflicting feelings or thoughts that are disturbing her at the moment."[22] Although most women are able to keep such anxieties in perspective, some cannot.

Research implies that certain young women, as well as men, suffer from a disorder known as muscle dysmorphia, in which a person believes that he or she is too weak, scrawny, or thin and must be more muscular. Dysmorphia is also known as bigorexia, or reverse anorexia nervosa. Sufferers—usually in their late teens—are sometimes obsessed with working out, are angry if they cannot, and typically monitor their protein intake religiously.

Even those who do not suffer from dysmorphia may be tempted to try steroids. While hours in the gym combined with a strict diet will make a person stronger, healthier, and bigger, steroids have a stark impact. "The difference between a natural body builder and a steroid user is phenomenal," says one bodybuilder. "Without steroids you could create a great physique, but never the size. It's easy to tell a steroid user from a natural body builder. The naturals never make the books."[23]

Big Business

As with so many illegal drugs, anabolic steroids are widely available to those looking to obtain them. Potential buyers talk to friends at the gym, seek out family members who take them, or, most commonly, go online and do a Google search. *Houston Chronicle* columnist John P. Lopez did just that in March 2005. His quick search for "buy steroids" yielded over 425,000 hits. Cyclist Stuart Stevens scored steroids at his local fitness center. Over the course of a few weeks, Stevens became friendly with another gym patron and soon found himself sitting in the guy's car, accepting a bottle of the steroid stanozolol. "'Where do you get this?' I said. 'A vet I know,' he answered casually. It took me a second to realize he meant veterinarian, not military veteran. 'Vets and Mexican pharmacists, that's where you get the best stuff.'"[24]

Because the laws regarding steroids vary so widely from country to country, acquiring the drugs is relatively easy. Journalist William Sherman decided to find out how easy it would be to buy steroids. "A few phone calls," writes Sherman, "and a . . . reporter quickly made two connections for $280 worth."[25]

The Internet also provides easy access to steroids. "A lot of people just get it over the Internet, so it really isn't out on the street as much as other drugs are,"[26] says Carlsbad, California, police sergeant Matt Margo, who oversees his department's vice and narcotics unit.

While steroids used for medical purposes typically require a prescription, a recent review of such Web sites suggests that most anabolic steroids have less strict requirements: "None of the steroid Web sites we reviewed required a prescription, and none used any sort of age verification service," states John Horton, president of LegitScript, an Internet pharmacy watchdog site. "Studies indicate that youth and young adults are the most at risk for illicit steroid use, and these Web sites are just a fraction of those we identified selling these drugs."[27]

> As with so many illegal drugs, anabolic steroids are widely available to those looking to obtain them.

Many sellers are able to get away with the sale of illegal steroids by calling them "supplements." But substituting an acceptable "s" word for one that is not can be a dangerous game. Many potential customers go online looking not for steroids but for dietary supplements—often in the form of powders—that will help them increase body mass through the addition of calories. Such products are widely available in local health food and vitamin stores. But a December 2007 study revealed that 13 of 52 supplements tested over a 6-month period contained traces of steroids banned by both the World Anti-Doping Agency and all of the major sports leagues. "Everything is a factor of dosage and duration, says doping expert Gary Wadler. If you're not being drug-tested, you could be consuming these supplements without knowing you're taking anabolic steroids. The risk to your health is real."[28]

How Serious a Problem Is Steroid Use?

66 Over the course of my five years at BYU (Brigham Young University), I have concrete proof of 13 to 15 guys [using steroids], and I would suspect others. And BYU is more temperate than most programs. I know other schools are worse. I would bet my house you could find at least five guys on every Division I team in the country (using steroids). 99

—Jason Scukanec, quoted in Luke Andrews, "Steroid Prevention the NCAA Way," CBS Sports, June 9, 2006. www.cstv.com.

Scukanec is a former lineman for BYU's football team.

66 Steroids are simply part of the game in the bodybuilding world, as common as barbells and a high protein diet. 99

—Kenny Wheeler, quoted in Edward Epstein, "Schwarzenegger Linked to Contests with Steroids," *San Francisco Chronicle*, October 1, 2003. www.sfgate.com.

Wheeler, a former professional bodybuilder, used steroids for 18 years.

* Editor's Note: While the definition of a primary source can be narrowly or broadly defined, for the purposes of Compact Research, a primary source consists of: 1) results of original research presented by an organization or researcher; 2) eyewitness accounts of events, personal experience, or work experience; 3) first-person editorials offering pundits' opinions; 4) government officials presenting political plans and/or policies; 5) representatives of organizations presenting testimony or policy.

66 They think, 'To go to college I have to have money. I'm working my tail off and not getting faster. I'm not going to do it that long, I'll get out of it.' Before you know it, it's out of control.99

—Mike Addorisio, quoted in Bonnie DiSimone, "Schools' Prevention Efforts Aim to Halt Rise of Steroid Use," *New York Times*, June 5, 2005. www.nytimes.com.

Addorisio is the track coach at Lyman Hall High School in Connecticut.

....

66 My whole priority was, I wanted people to say, 'That guy's huge.'99

—Craig, quoted in Cate Baily, "Behind the Bulk: Craig's Story," *Anabolic Steroids*, NIDA for Teens: The Science Behind Drug Abuse, 2003. http://teens.drugabuse.gov.

Craig abused steroids for five years until a receding hair line, chest pains, and family problems caused him to stop.

....

66 One of the greatest tragedies is Marion Jones serving time in jail. She's one of the greatest athletes in the history of the sport. She didn't need to dope. She had a natural gift.99

—Steven Ungerleider, quoted in Tim Christie, "To Catch a Cheat," *Eugene (OR) Register-Guard,* June 29, 2008.

A sports psychologist from Oregon, Ungerleider has researched doping among German athletes.

....

66 The benefit [of steroid use] is pretty clear. It enables you to get bigger. We live in a very vain society, a culture where beauty and fitness are at the top of almost everyone's list. But most people don't want to work to get there. They want to take the short cut. 99

—Roy Johnson, interviewed on *Tell Me More*, "Steroids' Appeal Reaches Beyond
Pro Athletes," National Public Radio, July 2, 2007. www.npr.org.

Johnson is editor of *Men's Fitness* magazine.

66 A conventional wisdom took over among the players that it would be difficult, in some cases impossible, to compete without anabolic substances. 99

—Howard Bryant, *Juicing the Game.* New York: Viking, 2005.

Bryant is a longtime sports writer for the *Boston Herald*.

66 When he was with the Pirates, [Barry] Bonds's body had been long and lean, a muscular version of a marathon runner's build. Now he had been transformed into an NFL linebacker, with broad shoulders, a wide chest, and huge biceps. 99

—Mark Fainaru-Wada and Lance Williams, *Game of Shadows: Barry Bonds, BALCO,
and the Steroids Scandal That Rocked Professional Sports.* New York: Gotham, 2006.

Fainaru-Wada and Williams are investigative reporters for the *San Francisco Chronicle*.

❝I wanted the body of a 25-year-old pro athlete at eighteen years old. What I didn't understand was that at 18, I was still growing.❞

—Jack, quoted in Association Against Steroid Abuse, "Anabolic Steroid Use in Adolescents and High Schools," 2007. www.steroidabuse.com.

Jack is a former Virginia Tech football player.

❝Black market sales of these drugs approach $1 billion annually. Although not physically addicting, steroids can become an "obsession" among teens who desire athletic success. Long-term users may spend up to $400 a week on steroids and may support their habit by dealing the drug.❞

—Larry J. Siegel, Brandon C. Welsh, and Joseph J. Senna, *Juvenile Delinquency*. Belmont, CA: Thomson Wadsworth, 2005.

Siegel and Welsh teach criminal justice at the University of Massachusetts; Senna, a former assistant district attorney, teaches at Northeastern University.

How Serious a Problem Is Steroid Use?

- More than **100** different types of anabolic steroids have been developed, and each requires a prescription to be used legally in the United States.

- In a 2005 survey **18.1 percent** of eighth graders, **29.7 percent** of tenth graders, and **39.7 percent** of twelfth graders reported that steroids were "fairly easy" or "very easy" to obtain.

- In a poll taken just before the 2008 Beijing Olympics, **35 percent** of sports fans said they were not suspicious about the use of performance-enhancing drugs when they see or hear about an athlete breaking a world record.

- **Twenty-two percent** of sports fans suspected record-breaking swimmers were taking performance-enhancing drugs.

- The American Heart Association has estimated that at least **50 percent** of all Division I college football players have used steroids over substantial periods of time.

- In 2006, nearly **3 percent** of male high school seniors had tried steroids, according to a national survey by the University of Michigan.

- According to a 2002 NIDA-funded study, **2.5 percent** of eighth graders, **3.5 percent** of tenth graders, and **4 percent** of twelfth graders had tried steroids.

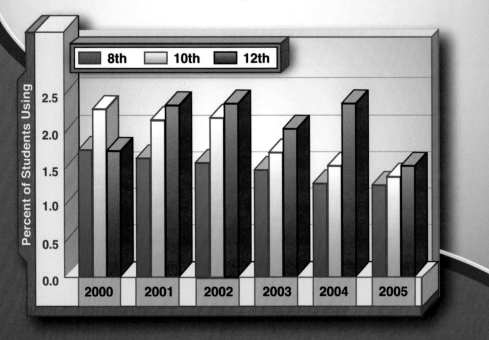

Steroids in School

Although steroids can be used by people of any age, educators and parents remain most concerned about young people trying them. The bar graph illustrates which students are most likely to seek steroids.

Source: NIDA, "Research Report Series," 2006. www.nida.nih.gov.

- According to a 2002 NIDA-funded study, approximately **30 percent** to **45 percent** of high school and college steroid users are not involved in competitive sports.

- According to Centers for Disease Control and Prevention (CDC) statistics, approximately **660,000** students between the ages of 14 and 17 had admitted using steroids.

- Studies show **four times** as many men abuse steroids as women, but the number of women is still significant.

Steroid Use Higher in Middle School than High School

These bar graphs show anabolic steroid use among males and females from early adolescence through late adolescence. In both cases, middle school students were more likely to take steroids. By high school, steroid use decreases.

Trends in Anabolic-Androgenic Steroid Use

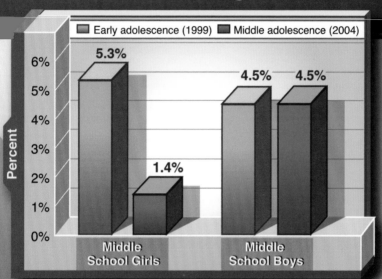

Early adolescence (1999) ■ Middle adolescence (2004)

- 5.3% Middle School Girls
- 1.4%
- 4.5% Middle School Boys
- 4.5%

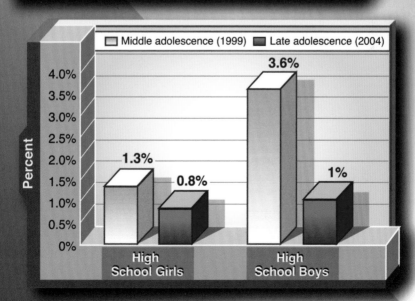

Middle adolescence (1999) ■ Late adolescence (2004)

- 1.3% High School Girls
- 0.8%
- 3.6% High School Boys
- 1%

Source: *Endocrine Today*, "Steroid Use Among Adolescents Unchanged from 1999 to 2004," April 1, 2007. www.endocrinetoday.com.

31

Commonly Used Steroids

Below are lists of the most commonly used steroids. Those listed on the left come in the form of a cream or a patch, which a person might wear on his or her leg or arm. Those on the right are typically injected directly into a muscle.

Oral Steroids	Injectable Steroids
• Anadrol (oxymetholone)	• Deca-Durabolin (nandrolone decanoate)
• Oxandrin (oxandrolone)	• Durabbolin (nandrolone phenpropionate)
• Dianabol (methandrostenolone)	• Depo-Testosterone (testosterone cypionate)
• WInstrol (stanolzolol)	• Equipoise (bodenone undecylenate)
	• Tetrahydrogestrinone (THG)

Source: NIDA, "Research Report Series," 2006. www.nida.nih.gov.

How Dangerous Are Steroids?

"His neck was so wide from using steroids, I just remember looking at him and going, 'Jeez.'"

—Emily Parker, *Dallas Morning News.*

"I'd gained 20 pounds. I had very bad acne. My voice was starting to change. I had a menstrual cycle every other week."

—Kelli White, *Louisville Courier-Journal.*

Stop by almost any gym or weight training facility in the United States and you will see them: bulky, sweating men and women with thick necks and rippling muscles. They grunt and groan as they bench-press hundreds of pounds above their heads; many stay in the gym for hours, day in and day out. While it is virtually impossible to know for certain who has "juiced" and who has not, for those taking the drugs the results can be startling. Adam Conn knows firsthand how steroids can change your look and your life. He started small and his mother was concerned. So were his doctors. His bones, they told him, were not growing normally. In seventh grade he weighed less than 70 pounds. Yet Adam wanted to wrestle. Under medical supervision, he began taking monthly injections of testosterone. The steroids made an impact:

> By the time wrestling season rolled around, I increased from 68 pounds the year before to 86 pounds (and this was a good thing, given that the lowest weight class for 9th grade was 92 pounds). That's a 26% increase. My body fat

was down to 3.2% (granted, it was never all that high before). I had larger-than-expected leg muscles for my size, and continued to work my legs in the weight room.[29]

Conn got bigger but suffered few of the adverse side effects often associated with steroid use. For him, steroids were a way of jump-starting his body's own internal processes. Still, for many other athletes, both male and female, using such illicit drugs can disrupt and even destroy a body's delicate balance.

Acne Scars and Hair Loss

In August 2008 German doctors released the graphic pictures of a 21-year-old bodybuilder's acne-scarred body. The first photograph shows a muscular, bronzed chest with a few traces of the acne. In shocking contrast, the second photo reveals the ulcerated and open sores suffered by the anonymous bodybuilder soon after.

> While it is virtually impossible to know for certain who has "juiced" and who has not, for those taking the drugs the results can be startling.

Antiseptic and antibiotic therapy helped heal the lifter's oozing wounds, but according to dermatologist Peter Arne Gerber, "It is questionable whether he will be able to start building muscle mass again—he may not be able to perform the exercises due to the scarring."[30] This extreme case made international news and served as a warning for those who take the risk of introducing steroids into their systems.

Acne is common among users and is caused by the hormonal imbalance brought on by steroids. Beyond that, says dermatologist Bruce Robinson, "Steroids increase the amount of sebum, or oil, production from the sebaceous gland, and acne is [caused by] a bacteria that thrives on the sebum."[31] Over-the-counter ointments as well as prescription drugs such as Accutane can reduce the outbreak of the red and blotchy onset of acne brought on by steroids, but these medications can have their own side effects. And despite the danger of permanent scarring, most steroid users appear willing to take the risk.

Premature balding is another gamble male steroid users seem willing to take. Steroids accelerate hair loss in men who have a family background, or genetic predisposition, for baldness.

David Jacobs, an admitted dealer of human growth hormone and steroids, says he sold the substances to a small group of NFL players, who then passed them on to teammates. "The excuse they did it under was that the players were losing their hair because they were taking their helmets on and off,"[32] says Jacobs. He strongly suspects that human growth hormone (HGH), which the NFL does not test for, was behind the abrupt baldness epidemic.

Steroids have a somewhat different effect on women. While they, too, may experience hair loss on their heads, they may also find hair sprouting on their faces.

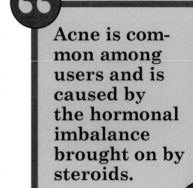

> Acne is common among users and is caused by the hormonal imbalance brought on by steroids.

Hormonal Upheaval

While acne and baldness can affect a person's looks and, perhaps, his or her self-esteem, such side effects are unlikely to bring long-term consequences. For former athlete Andreas Krieger, state-mandated steroid injections literally changed his life. Krieger was born a girl named Heidi in East Germany in 1966.

In the mid-1970s East Germany felt a fierce sense of competition, especially with the United States, and was willing to win at any cost. As many as 10,000 athletes, including Krieger, were fed massive doses of anabolic steroids as part of their training regimen. By age 16 Krieger was receiving blue pills wrapped in tin foil—vitamins, her coaches told her. In fact, she was ingesting Oral-Turinabol, an anabolic steroid. In short order, Heidi's clothes stopped fitting her and she bulked up to 220 pounds of testosterone-fueled muscle. Despite her manly physique, the 18-year-old found her niche in the shot put competition. "I got the feeling that I belonged. That's what I wanted, to belong. . . . I had worked hard. To question whether these were hormones I was being given, I didn't ask or suspect."[33]

The results of Heidi's gradual transformation included a gold medal in the 1986 World Championships, but the strain of almost constant weight training soon took its toll on Heidi's knees, back, and hips. By 1991 her athletic career was finished. She remained in denial that steroids had any part in her physical metamorphosis, but she did feel an increasing sense of isolation and depression, and at one point seriously considered suicide. But, over a number of years, the inner turmoil gave way to a grudging acceptance that steroids had indeed forced the changes in her body.

> **Doctors are certain that steroids disrupt the natural cell development in a person's body.**

To complete the process, Heidi had a double mastectomy and tried to move on in life as a man named Andreas. These many years later, Andreas tries to put his former life in perspective. "I have to accept that Heidi is part of my history," Andreas says. "The more open I am, the less problems I have. Less than if I try to deny her."[34]

Such extreme hormonal changes as experienced by Krieger are rare, but doctors are certain that steroids disrupt the natural cell development in a person's body. While female users typically may see a reduction in breast size, males will develop larger breasts. A male's testicles will often shrink; a woman's clitoris usually swells, and her menstrual cycle can become erratic; male sperm count decreases and, as a result, so does fertility.

Teen Danger

Krieger began ingesting anabolic steroids as a teenager, a stage of development during which steroid use is particularly dangerous. Statistics show that teen interest in steroids continues into the present day, especially in middle school; students will "stack" steroids to achieve desired results. Stacking occurs when a person uses two or three or more performance-enhancing drugs to get better results in a shorter amount of time.

Teens' bodies are more fragile than those of adults. During the hormonal upheaval of puberty, steroids can dangerously interfere with the development of reproductive organs and bone growth as well as worsen side effects such as acne. Dionne Passacantando, a cheerleader and gymnast from Allen, Texas, now living in New Jersey, paid a severe price for trying them.

Her quest for the six-pack abdominal muscles of her dreams seemed reasonable enough. Dionne wanted to look good, to become what she saw in the tabloids at the supermarket. "It's this whole Hollywood thing," she says. "Everyone is so affected by movie stars and that whole pop culture thing. I think it takes over a little bit. . . . Everybody has their own quarrels with self-esteem and self-image, and that's what every young woman goes through."[35] Dionne's quest for the perfect body was nothing new. As a gymnast, she knew the routine: stay thin, sometimes by starving herself, or eating and then throwing up. But steroids were new and, she remembers, easier to buy than beer.

But Dionne's growing body complicated matters, hormonally. While she added 10 pounds of muscle to her thin frame, for the first time in her life she suffered from severe depression and a state of severe anger and aggression commonly known as "roid rage." Doctors say "roid rage" often occurs once testosterone levels subside after steroid use is stopped. For Dionne, it got worse when she attempted suicide and two days later got drunk in her car after a fight with her boyfriend. "In that inebriation, I did have a moment of clarity and thought, 'I can't do this anymore,'" she says. "I'm driving around drunk, I could hurt other people. Something made me say, 'I need to take myself to the hospital, I need some help.'"[36] Dionne entered a treatment facility and, in time, got clean.

Although Dionne's story might serve as a warning for some teenagers considering steroids, a recent statistic suggests that 57 percent of high school steroid users would risk living a shorter life if the steroids increased their athletic performance.

> " During the hormonal upheaval of puberty, steroids can dangerously interfere with the development of reproductive organs and bone growth as well as worsen side effects such as acne. "

Heartsick, Liver Sore

A 2004 study revealed that those who took anabolic steroids were 2.5 times more likely to suffer from the symptoms of heart disease than those who did not. But without more knowledge of those studied—diet, frequency of exercise—researchers find it difficult to make a direct link between the two. One anabolic steroid, EPO, is known to increase red blood cells and may cause the blood to thickly clot, which could lead to strokes and heart attacks.

Steroids are also known to take a toll on the liver. As the largest gland in the human body, the liver produces an alkaline compound known as bile, which aids in the digestion of food. Steroids retard liver function and can cause bleeding cysts and, in rare cases, liver cancer.

In only 16 weeks, Canadian novelist Craig Davidson went from flabby to fit taking daily doses of steroids, but he says the drugs destroyed his body, especially his internal organs. "The blood tests showed my liver values were totally out of whack."[37] Unlike some of the symptoms resulting from steroid use, damage to the liver can be permanent and debilitating.

> " A recent statistic suggests that 57 percent of high school steroid users would risk living a shorter life if the steroids increased their performance. "

Emotional Rollercoaster

When pro wrestler Chris Benoit killed his wife and 7-year-old son and then himself in 2007, the media immediately wondered whether illegal steroids had played a part in Benoit's murderous rampage.

Upon arrival at the family home in Fayetteville, Georgia, police investigators discovered a variety of prescription drugs, including anabolic steroids. Benoit and his wife, Nancy, had a history of marital problems, but the viciousness of the murders still shocked the southern community.

CNN's chief medical correspondent, neurosurgeon Sanjay Gupta, speculates on the cause: "The drugs said to be found in the home are a synthetic form of testosterone," he says. "A lot of people use it to build muscle mass, but there are longstanding known relationships between the steroids and roid rage. It could lead to psychosis and anti-social behavior and depression."[38]

An autopsy on Benoit later confirmed suspicions voiced by members of the media and the wrestling community. At the time of his death, the WWE star's urine had 207 milligrams of testosterone per liter, 40 percent above what is considered normal. Although investigators cannot be certain, it is likely that Benoit's massive consumption of steroids contributed to his homicidal fury.

Former bodybuilder Matt Alavi knows the aggression that comes from taking steroids. He lived it. Alavi became a devoted juicer at the age of 23 and soon noticed how unpredictable his moods became. His emotions boiled close to the surface until one day, "I was pissed with my roommate who started me on steroids. . . . I got the urge to just punch him in the head. But instead I punched a hole in the George Foreman grill and shattered that. I was thinking look what I've done to myself with this crap!"[39]

> " One anabolic steroid, EPO, is known to increase red blood cells and may cause the blood to thickly clot, which could lead to strokes and heart attacks. "

Can Steroids Lead to Death?

Death from taking steroids is a rare but not unheard of occurrence. Some reports have claimed that the mood swings often associated with the drugs can lead to suicidal thoughts. Because excessive use has been linked to cancer as well as liver and heart disease, many physicians are convinced steroids can kill a person. Since 1997 at least seven professional wrestlers have died in steroid-related incidents.

In 1992 former football star Lyle Alzado told *Sports Illustrated* he believed his frequent steroid injections caused his inoperable brain cancer. Alzado revealed that he began taking steroids in 1969 and never truly stopped. He played for 15 seasons in the National Football League, twice making All-Pro; Alzado was big, strong, and tough, and he instilled fear in many of his opponents. But, he said, "Look at me now. I wobble when I walk and sometimes have to hold onto somebody. You have to give me time to answer questions, because I have trouble remembering things."[40] Alzado never lived to prove a direct link between the massive doses of performance-enhancing drugs he took and his cancer. He died on May 14, 1992, at age 43.

While experts have never verified Alzado's claims that steroids caused his brain cancer, a majority of doctors are certain that steroids are dangerous to the human body. But steroids are often taken in secret, so it may be years before researchers can truly determine the long-term damage steroids have done.

Primary Source Quotes*

How Dangerous Are Steroids?

❝I played with fire and got burned. . . . I am paying for it now.❞

> —Doug the Demon Man, "My Personal Story," Anabolics Mall, 2005. www.anabolicsmall.com.

Doug, an avid bodybuilder, began entering bodybuilding competitions in the early 1980s.

❝Steroids have been labeled bad because people abuse them. . . . Grown men can take steroids without too many side effects at all because we are not producing the same amount of testosterone anymore. We are replacing what should already be there. Older women take estrogen all the time so what's the difference if an older man takes testosterone?❞

> —jjoe0990, in ConvinceMe...Start a Debate, "Steroids Good vs. Bad," February 3, 2007. www.convinceme.net.

jjoe0990's blog on the "Steroids Good" side of a debate hosted by the Web site ConvinceMe.

* Editor's Note: While the definition of a primary source can be narrowly or broadly defined, for the purposes of Compact Research, a primary source consists of: 1) results of original research presented by an organization or researcher; 2) eyewitness accounts of events, personal experience, or work experience; 3) first-person editorials offering pundits' opinions; 4) government officials presenting political plans and/or policies; 5) representatives of organizations presenting testimony or policy.

Primary Source Quotes

"If today's athletes say they want to take the risk, they really don't know what risk they are taking."

—Andreas Krieger, quoted in CNN, "Athlete Says Sports Steroids Changed Him from Woman to Man, August 11, 2008. www.cnn.com.

Krieger, the former Heidi Krieger, a world champion female shot-putter, is convinced that steroids changed his physique into that of a man.

"It was almost like I was like a heroin addict. It got to the point where I needed the injection to work out, to feel good about myself."

—Chris Wash, quoted in "Teens & Steroids: A Dangerous Mix," CBS News, June 3, 2004. www.cbsnews.com.

Wash, a former high school basketball player, began taking steroids at the age of 15.

"Prolonged steroid use may be particularly harmful to young people. Premature fusion of the long bones from steroids use can result in stunted growth in adolescents and pre adolescents."

—William N. Taylor, *Anabolic Steroids and the Athlete*. Jefferson, NC: McFarland, 2002.

Taylor is a writer and physician.

66 Suddenly we were growing beards and things got really bad after the Olympics. I became really aggressive, probably because we weren't being doped any more. Now I know that this was also a withdrawal symptom. 99

—Katharina Bullin, quoted in PBS, "Secrets of the Dead: Doping for Gold," transcript, PBS, May 14, 2008. www.pbs.org.

Bullin is a former East German Olympian in volleyball.

66 Even if steroids weren't dangerous at all, it's still dangerous to rely on a drug for the way you feel about yourself or your performance. 99

—Chris Bell, interviewed on *Talk of the Nation*, "Are Steroids as 'American as Apple Pie?'" National Public Radio, June 12, 2008.

Bell is a former steroid user.

66 The most frightening result of the steroid debate is that it may be teaching youth to cheat. 99

—Nathan Jendrick, *Dunks, Doubles, Doping*. Guilford, CT: Lyons, 2006.

Jendrick is an author and personal fitness trainer.

66 Most guys would stack different drugs together for the most effect, either trying to gain or lose massive amounts of weight, depending on the time of year. We began to add other drugs to prevent the side effects. Some of the guys even started using cocaine to get charged up before games. 99

—"Jason," quoted in ABC News, "Youth and Steroids: A Deadly Combination," April 10, 2007. www.abcnews.go.com.

Jason, who chose not to use his real name, began taking anabolic steroids as a freshman in high school.

Facts and Illustrations

How Dangerous Are Steroids?

- In a recent study of 88 athletes who used steroids, **23 percent** reported "major mood disturbances" including mania and major depression.

- During 2005, **56.8 percent** of twelfth graders surveyed reported that using steroids was a "great risk."

- Health consequences that can occur in both males and females include liver **cancer**, heart attacks, and **elevated cholesterol** levels.

- In addition to the physical effects, anabolic steroids can also cause increased irritability and **aggression**.

- Some steroid abusers experience **withdrawal symptoms** when they stop taking the drug, including mood swings, fatigue, restlessness, loss of appetite, insomnia, reduced sex drive, and depression.

- Steroid use can cause the **testicles to shrink** as well as decrease mental and physical activity.

- Steroid use among adolescents may prematurely stop the lengthening of bones, resulting in **stunted growth**.

- **Six percent** of students in grades nine through 12 admitted taking steroid pills or shots without a doctor's prescription one or more

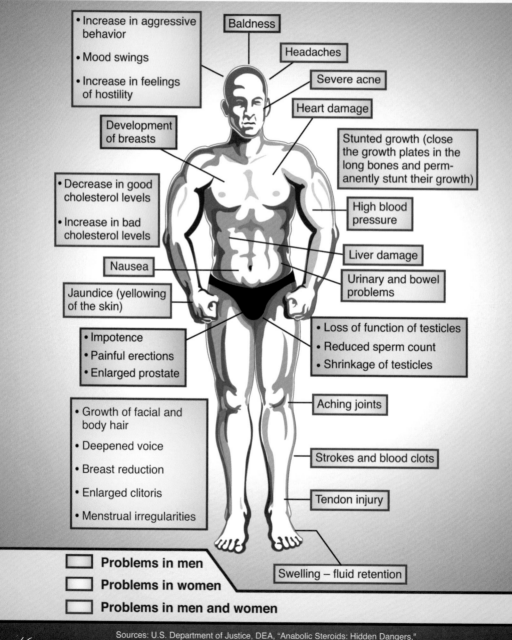

Side Effects of Steroids in Men and Women

Additional testosterone in a male's body will increase muscle mass and strength, but other, unwanted side effects will often occur. The introduction of synthetic male hormones into the body of a woman can also result in a variety of unwanted side effects.

- Increase in aggressive behavior
- Mood swings
- Increase in feelings of hostility

Baldness

Headaches

Severe acne

Heart damage

Development of breasts

Stunted growth (close the growth plates in the long bones and perm-anently stunt their growth)

High blood pressure

- Decrease in good cholesterol levels
- Increase in bad cholesterol levels

Liver damage

Nausea

Urinary and bowel problems

Jaundice (yellowing of the skin)

- Impotence
- Painful erections
- Enlarged prostate

- Loss of function of testicles
- Reduced sperm count
- Shrinkage of testicles

- Growth of facial and body hair
- Deepened voice
- Breast reduction
- Enlarged clitoris
- Menstrual irregularities

Aching joints

Strokes and blood clots

Tendon injury

Swelling – fluid retention

Problems in men
Problems in women
Problems in men and women

Sources: U.S. Department of Justice, DEA, "Anabolic Steroids: Hidden Dangers," March 2008; *USA Today*, "How Anabolic Steroids Work," www.usatoday.com.

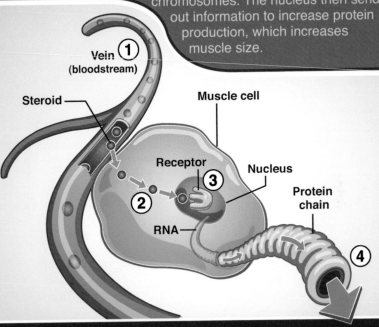

How Steroids Build Muscle

A steroid builds mass by being carried by the blood toward the muscle's cell walls where it attaches to a receptor. The steroid then enters the cell nucleus where it interacts with chromosomes. The nucleus then sends out information to increase protein production, which increases muscle size.

Vein ① (bloodstream)

Steroid

Muscle cell

Receptor

Nucleus

③

②

Protein chain

RNA

④

Source: Dan Raley, "How an Aberdeen Garage Became Key Stop in Global Steroid Pipeline," *Seattle Post-Intelligener* October 29, 2007. http://seattlepi.nwsource.com.

times. The data, which was collected from 1999 to 2003, showed a substantial increase from the **3.7 percent** reported in 1999.

- A recent study of 227 men admitted to a private treatment center for dependence on heroin or similar drugs found that **9.3 percent** had abused anabolic steroids before trying any other illicit drug.

  - Of these, **86 percent** first used heroin or similar drugs to counter-act insomnia and irritability resulting from the steroids.

The Route of Illegal Steroids

Although anabolic steroids are illegal in the United States, other countries produce and sell them to, among others, American consumers, who secretly buy them from drug dealers or even friends. This map follows the route of steroids, as the raw powder makes its way from a factory in Beijing, China, to Aberdeen, Washington, where Samar Labs—a small private company—refines the powder into pills. After manufacture, the steroids are secretly shipped to Las Vegas, Nevada, where GA Labs sells them on the Internet or through other channels.

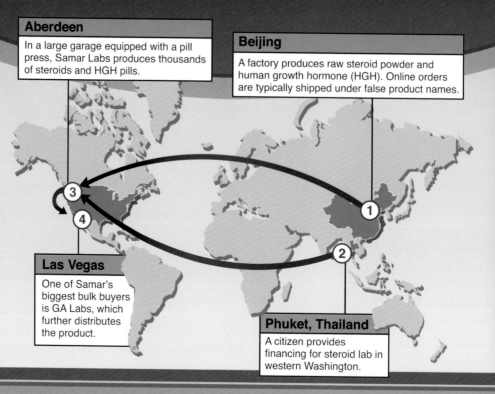

Aberdeen
In a large garage equipped with a pill press, Samar Labs produces thousands of steroids and HGH pills.

Beijing
A factory produces raw steroid powder and human growth hormone (HGH). Online orders are typically shipped under false product names.

Las Vegas
One of Samar's biggest bulk buyers is GA Labs, which further distributes the product.

Phuket, Thailand
A citizen provides financing for steroid lab in western Washington.

Source: Dan Raley, "How an Aberdeen Garage Became Key Stop in Global Steroid Pipeline," *Seattle Post-Intelligencer*, October 29, 2007. http://seattlepi.nwsource.com.

- Anabolic steroid doses taken by abusers can be **10 to 100 times higher** than the doses used for medical conditions.

Should Steroid Testing and Laws Be Strengthened?

> ❝One thing that is clear is we have become increasingly better at detecting things. Things athletes have gotten away with in the past are much more difficult to get away with.❞
>
> —Physician and self-proclaimed "steroid detective," Gary Wadler.

> ❝The big issue with results is: Are we seeing less positives because doping is cleaned up, or because athletes have gotten smarter and moved on to other drugs?❞
>
> —UCLA chemist Don Catlin.

In September 2007 the Drug Enforcement Administration (DEA) of the United States announced the results of Operation Raw Deal. The steroid sting, years in the making, resulted in 124 arrests and the seizure of 56 alleged drug labs, not to mention the collection of millions of units of steroids. Seven federal agencies, as well as nine countries, helped do the work. DEA administrator Karen Tandy spoke glowingly of the outcome: "DEA successfully attacked the illegal steroid industry at every level of its distribution network."[41]

The rules and regulations governing the use of steroids and other performance-enhancing drugs have evolved over the years and are now more stringent than ever before. After Congress passed the Anabolic Steroids Control Act of 1990, possession of the drugs became punishable with a $1,000 fine and up to one year in prison. Yet pick up any newspaper and a reader is bound to find fresh cases of steroid use and abuse almost every day. Despite the federal effort and thousands of education programs across the country, the problem of illegal anabolic steroids only seems to grow.

Taking the Test

Testing methods have changed little in the last 30 years: A person urinates into a plastic cup, the contents of which are then analyzed in a laboratory. On average, 100,000 drug tests are taken by amateur and professional athletes each year at a cost of more than $30 million.

The tests are meant to work in two ways: first, as a drug detection system, and second, as a deterrent. The idea, officials claim, is to put athletes on notice that doping will not be tolerated, thus ensuring fairness for all who compete.

> " The rules and regulations governing the use of steroids and other performance-enhancing drugs have evolved over the years and are now more stringent than ever before. "

Today, testing is required in many school districts across the country. Yet the $175 cost per steroid screening can be a burden when federal and local school funding is already tight. A recent study showed that of the 75 public school districts in the Dallas, Texas, area, only 8 tested for steroids. None of them tested year-round, which experts agree is essential in detecting various types of performance-enhancing drugs.

Testing is only one part of the solution. No test is unbeatable, and athletes looking for a way to boost their game often move in a secretive world where coaches, trainers, and teammates look the other way.

Beating the Test

In the 1980s and 1990s Victor Conte became known as the steroid supplier to the stars. As the founder of BALCO (Bay Area Laboratory Co-Operative) he reaped millions of dollars for his efforts and perfected the art of juicing without detection. Olympic athletes especially had to be prepared for anything when it came to testing for performance-enhancing drugs. The International Olympic Committee (IOC) policy allowed testers to ask for urine samples at any time of the day or night, often showing up at an athlete's home unannounced.

Conte's solution was to offer athletes "a broad menu of drugs that were difficult to detect,"[42] write journalists Mark Fainaru-Wada and Lance Williams in their book *Game of Shadows*. These included human growth hormone; EPO; norbolethone, also known as the Clear; and modafinil, a drug typically prescribed to combat narcolepsy.

Beating the doping test has become an obsession for many athletes. Only 8 days before the opening of the 2008 Olympic Games in Beijing, China, 7 female Russian athletes were suspended for violating doping rules. Each was a respected member of the track team, including sprinter Yelena Soboleva, winner of the silver medal in the 1,500-meter race at the 2004 games in Athens, Greece. The International Association of Athletics Federations (IAAF) caught the women switching their tainted urine samples for ones free of steroids.

> " No test is unbeatable, and athletes looking for a way to boost their game often move in a secretive world where coaches, trainers, and teammates look the other way. "

The Chinese tried to avoid such embarrassment, since they were hosting the games. "We have a very clear goal for our Chinese athletes, and that is for no positive doping cases to occur during the Olympics," said antidoping agency director Du Lijun. "This agency doesn't care about how many gold medals we have. The most important thing for us is to maintain a good image."[43] But such noble ideals have not always been considered vital, and testing remains an imperfect method of detection.

False Positives

Less than perfect methods of evaluation are a natural consequence of testing so many athletes, especially during enormous events such as the Olympics. But some athletes complain that untrue allegations, even after being proven untrue, can ruin their careers and cost them millions of dollars in endorsement deals. Mike Lowell, 2007 World Series MVP, helped lead the Boston Red Sox to a championship. His is a respected voice in Major League Baseball, in part because he has never been accused of taking steroids, nor has he ever failed a drug test.

Lowell remains suspicious of the drug-testing methods now currently in place because they can lead to false positives. "If it's 93 percent accurate, that's going to be seven false positives," the Red Sox third baseman says. "Ninety-three percent is 70 guys. That's almost three whole rosters. You're destroying someone's reputation. What if one of the false positives is [Hall of Famer] Cal Ripken? Doesn't it put a black mark on his career?"[44]

> **Baseball is not the only sport to be tainted by the specter of illegal steroids.**

While stories of false-positive steroid tests are rare—and often little more than rumors—many professional athletes agree than even an accusation of steroid use when actually innocent is too risky. "I believe a false positive is a remote possibility at best," says Boston pitcher Curt Schilling, "but it's very clear now that if someone is a positive they're done. They might still be able to play after the suspension, but they are forever labeled as a cheater."[45]

For Schilling and others, their livelihoods depend on accuracy in testing and could be compromised if officials do not take care to ensure the integrity of the process. But baseball is not the only sport to be tainted by the specter of illegal steroids.

The Tour de France

The regulations for professional cycling are as tough as baseball's, yet the sport remains a hotbed of doping activity. Cycling's premier event, the Tour de France, has been held every summer since 1903. Considered one of the most grueling competitions in all of sports, the 23-day, 21-stage event winds its way through much of the Gallic countryside before ending in Paris. Riders cover 2,200 miles (3,500 km), much of it through mountainous terrain, stopping each evening to rest their weary bodies. The prize, worth millions of dollars to the winning team, has tempted cyclists into questionable behavior almost since the beginning.

Early competitors admitted, or were found guilty of, taking substances such as cocaine, strychnine, chloroform, and aspirin. In 1967

British cyclist Tom Simpson died from the apparently lethal combination of amphetamine and thirst. But a turning point in the history of the race came in 1998, when French law enforcement raided hotel rooms of the Festina team and discovered caches of EPO, HGH, testosterone, and amphetamine. After this "Tour of Shame," as it was called, the International Cycling Union (ICU) put in place better methods for doping detection, including testing after each stage of the race. Nonetheless, rumors and positive tests persisted. Seven-time Tour de France winner Lance Armstrong, often accused of doping, especially by the European press, has never tested positive for foreign substances and remains a cycling icon.

Another American rider was not so fortunate. Floyd Landis, from Lancaster County, Pennsylvania, won the 2007 Tour in stunning, come-from-behind fashion in the seventeenth leg of the contest. Like all tour leaders, Landis donned a yellow jersey, eventually riding to victory down the Champs-Élysées in Paris.

But soon after, Landis tested positive for having higher than normal levels of testosterone in his system. Landis denied using the hormone, but a backup sample confirmed the initial test. Tour organizers quickly withdrew Landis's title and gave it to second-place finisher, Oscar Pereiro.

Landis's court appeal was rejected, and the doping charges against him stuck. The laws governing cycling had worked, and ICU president Pat McQuaid felt vindicated: "We're very happy with the result because the testing system was put under intense scrutiny by what you would call a celebrated group of lawyers, some of the best in America, and it stood up under that scrutiny. Now he [Landis] can keep the yellow jersey, put it on his wall and dream about it, but Oscar Pereiro is now the winner."[46]

> " Seven-time Tour de France winner Lance Armstrong, often accused of doping, especially by the European press, has never tested positive for foreign substances and remains a cycling icon. "

Cracking Down

Only in the last two decades have sports leagues and athletic associations like the ICU seriously cracked down on those seeking to gain an unfair advantage through the use of synthetic substances. In 1990 the National Football League (NFL) instituted a year-round, random steroid testing program, becoming the first major sports league to do so. Three years later the Association of Tennis Professionals, the Women's Tennis Association, and the International Tennis Federation got into the act by organizing an antidoping program. The National Basketball Association (NBA) banned steroids in 1999. But this self-policing is not always effective nor timely.

> One recent study taken in 2005 and 2006 and involving more than 3,200 students in 12 states suggests that young people often become interested in steroids by watching their athletic idols.

In the case of Major League Baseball (MLB), only after a public outcry and a great deal of media scrutiny did the league move to act. Until 2002 the league had no standing policy on steroid testing. Not until 2004 was testing for players made mandatory. And this was only after a scandal that rocked the world of professional sports. On September 3, 2003, government agents raided the offices of Victor Conte's BALCO, seizing records of the company's clients. BALCO promoted itself as a nutrition center. In reality, the company was supplying athletes with illegal substances. Among those listed as BALCO clients were baseball players Jason Giambi, Gary Sheffield, and emerging slugger Barry Bonds.

In 2005 baseball agreed to ban steroids. Initially, the penalties were less than strict: first positive, 10 days suspension; second, 30 days; third, 60 days; fourth, one year. More recently, the penalties have been increased: a first positive result bans a player for 50 games; a second offense bars him from 100 games; a third positive test results in a lifetime ban.

Whether the threat of such severe punishment will deter players from using steroids or other illegal substances remains to be seen. But Penn

State professor Charles Yesalis has his doubts: "Whether it is in combat, business, sports, or even marriage, trying to gain an advantage is a no-brainer. It is an innate human trait."[47]

But others disagree. One recent study made in 2005 and 2006 involved more than 3,200 students in 12 states and suggests that young people often become interested in steroids by watching their athletic idols. Of those surveyed, 57 percent said that professional athletes influenced their decision to use the drugs.

It remains an open question: Will more or better testing stop the use of steroids in professional sports or in the public at large? No definitive conclusion has been reached. But athletic officials are certain of one thing:

> **Will more or better testing stop the use of steroids in professional sports or in the public at large?**

Failing to test for steroids and being less stringent about the rules against them would do permanent damage to the idea of fairness and honesty in athletic competition.

Primary Source Quotes*

Should Steroid Testing and Laws Be Strengthened?

❝ It was systematic doping, it was cheating and, you know what, there are consequences when you cheat. ❞

— Wendy Boglioli, quoted in PBS, "Secrets of the Dead: Doping for Gold," transcript, May 14, 2008. www.pbs.org.

Boglioli won gold and bronze medals in swimming at the 1976 Olympic Games in Montreal, Canada.

❝ What is wrong with just letting 'the show,' as players call the major leagues, be a show—and not worrying about what goes on backstage? ❞

— Abraham Socher, "No Game for Old Men," *Commentary,* March 2008.

Socher teaches at Oberlin College in Ohio.

Bracketed quotes indicate conflicting positions.

* Editor's Note: While the definition of a primary source can be narrowly or broadly defined, for the purposes of Compact Research, a primary source consists of: 1) results of original research presented by an organization or researcher; 2) eyewitness accounts of events, personal experience, or work experience; 3) first-person editorials offering pundits' opinions; 4) government officials presenting political plans and/or policies; 5) representatives of organizations presenting testimony or policy.

❝Nobody is providing justification for those people who violate the WADA [World Anti-Doping Agency] rules. It is clear that there is some percentage of athletes that do this in spite of everything, and not only in Russia.❞

—Gennady V. Shvets, quoted in Jeré Longman, "Russian Olympians Suspended for Doping Violations," *New York Times,* August 1, 2008. www.nytimes.com.

Shvets heads the Russian Olympic Committee press service.

❝Steroids were used before they were illegal, and they'll continue to be used. So why not just legalize it? Tax the steroids heavily instead of letting foreign markets reap in the trade, and order that a physician assists the user so that side effects are minimized.❞

—Stephen Catanese, "There . . . I Said It: Are Steroids Good for Sports?" *Penn,* March 30, 2007. http://media.www.thepenn.org.

Catanese is a graduate of the University of Pennsylvania in Philadelphia.

❝It's hard to say that steroids were good for baseball but there were a lot of positive things that came out of it. The great thing about baseball though is that it always survives. . . . And with a little assist from steroids, baseball was able to overcome one of the darkest periods to face the game. In the end, maybe steroids did a little more good than harm.❞

—Brian Joseph, "Steroids: Good for the Game?" *Baseball Digest Daily,* March 22, 2008. http://seamheads.com.

Joseph is a freelance sportswriter.

66 Detection of anabolic steroid misuse poses particular problems, particularly since the steroids can be taken prior to competition, allowing a 'washout' period before competing. 99

—David R. Mottram, *Drugs in Sport*. London: Taylor and Francis, 2005.

Mottram is an expert on doping in sports.

66 There comes a time when it becomes a burden. Sometimes it feels like an infringement on athletes' rights, that we're being confined, that it's unfair. 99

—Gabe Jennings, quoted in Tim Christie, "To Catch a Cheat," *Eugene (OR) Register-Guard*, June 29, 2008.

Jennings, a middle distance runner, competed in the Olympic trials for the Beijing 2008 games.

66 We have to find the national will to test for performance-enhancing drugs at the level at which the greatest numbers compete, at the level at which kids are being told every day that if they get bigger and stronger, they can make it to the next step on the climb to superstardom. 99

—Mike Celizic, "Time for Steroid Testing in High School," NBC Sports, April 24, 2004. www.msnbc.msn.com.

Celizic is a contributing writer for MSNBC.

❝If you test positive for something, many people aren't interested in your truth. They're only interested in the positive drug test.❞

—Max Jaben, quoted in Ryan Young, "Olympic Qualifier Jaben Tests Positive for Steroids; Trip to Beijing in Doubt," *Kansas City (MO) Star,* July 18, 2008.

Jaben, a world-class freestyle swimmer, was ousted from the Israeli Olympic team after twice failing drug tests.

....

❝We don't think we need to stiffen our penalties. Let Congress act if they want to. We have put a responsible model in place. We didn't need Congress to tell us to put it in, so why would we need them to modify it?❞

—Gene Upshaw, quoted in "MLB Steroid Law 'Minimum' Standard," CBS News, November 17, 2005. www.cbsnews.com.

Upshaw, who died in August 2008, was a pro football Hall of Fame guard and executive director of the NFL Players Association.

....

Should Steroid Testing and Laws Be Strengthened?

- According to 2006 statistics, only **4 of the 11,217** student-athletes who were screened nationwide tested positive for steroids.

- It costs approximately **$105 per athlete** for each steroid test.

- A Minnesota law passed in 2005 calls for a maximum **20-year prison sentence** for the sale of performance-enhancing drugs to minors.

- According to the 1991 Controlled Substances Act (CSA), it is illegal in the United States to possess or sell anabolic steroids without a **valid prescription**.

- Possession of steroids is a federal offense punishable by up to **one year in prison** and/or a minimum fine of **$1,000**.

- One West Virginia county tests **2 percent** of its high school athletes for steroids each week.

- The International Olympic Committee, National Collegiate Athletic Association, and many professional sports leagues have **banned the use of steroids** by athletes.

- Anabolic steroid **test results are confidential** and may be disclosed only to the student-athlete and the student-athlete's parents and the activity directors, principal, and assistant principals of the school attended by the student-athlete.

• According to state regulations student-athletes found to be positive for an anabolic steroid for the first time, or who refuse to submit to testing after random selection, face a **30-day suspension** from athletic competition.

Home Runs Steadily Increasing

This graph illustrates the tremendous increase in home runs in Major League Baseball from 1900 to 2010. While the home runs per at-bats percentage remained steady for the first 20 years of the century, players soon began knocking more balls out of the park in fewer tries. By the late twentieth century, home run production had skyrocketed, and continues to. At least part of this increase may be due to the use of anabolic steroids and other performance-enhancing substances.

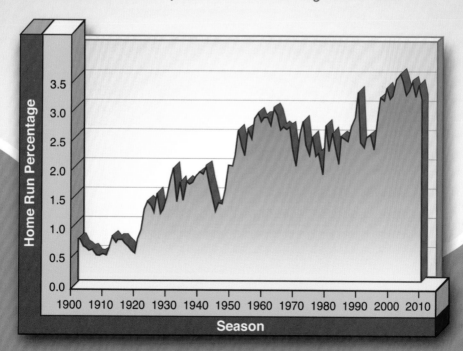

Source: David Pinto, "Utley's Homer Surge Could End 82-Year Drought," *Sporting News*, April 23, 2008. www.sportingnews.com.

- A recent New Jersey steroid testing program produced **1 positive result** in 500 urine samples.

- Florida recently administered 600 drug tests from a pool of 651 high schools at a cost to taxpayers of **$100,000**.

- The largest steroid testing program in the world, costing **$6 million**, will administer **6,000 tests** at approximately 400 Texas high schools.

Steroid Labs in the United States

In September 2007, Drug Enforcement Administration officials revealed the results of an 18-month investigation into the nation's illegal anabolic steroid industry. The states colored blue are the ones in which DEA agents conducted their inquiry. In all, 56 labs were seized in the dragnet.

States where steroid investigations took place

Source: Nicole Beyer, "E.V. Men Arrested in Steroid Sting," *East Valley Tribune*, September 24, 2007. www.eastvalleytribune.com.

Major League Baseball Penalties for Steroid Use

This chart compares the previous and current penalties for professional baseball players who break the league's rules on performance-enhancing drugs, including anabolic steroids.

OFFENSE	(Suspension in days)	
	OLD	NEW
First	None*	50
Second	15	100
Third	25	Lifetime ban
*Treatment		
Note: All suspensions are without pay		

Source: Harry Bruinius, "Will Steroids Alter Baseball Records, Too?" *Christian Science Monitor*, March 24, 2005. www.csmonitor.com.

How Can Steroid Use Be Prevented?

❝ I don't think any country is immune. China went through periods of doping in the 90s. In the old days it was East Germany. The U.S. has had its problems lately. No country wants a national athlete to test positive.❞

—David Howman, director general of the World Anti-Doping Agency.

❝ This is a problem that is not likely to go away in the near future. However, there are ways to reduce use among the most vulnerable people, our children . . . prevention programs that work to reduce anabolic steroid use among children and adolescents.❞

—Linn Goldberg, sports medicine specialist.

Many sportswriters have compared Major League Baseball's first scandal with its latest, steroid-connected one. In 1919, the Chicago White Sox played the Cincinnati Reds in the World Series. Yet the best of nine series was forever tainted when several Sox players conspired with gamblers to lose the games on purpose.

Forever after known as the Black Sox scandal, it would be another 86 years before the Sox finally redeemed themselves and won another championship. The explosive allegations of steroid use in the late 1990s and early 2000s rocked baseball in much the same way the Sox scandal had. Fans, especially, questioned their love of a game in such moral disrepair. Yet in both episodes, baseball and the world at large had the opportunity to learn from the bitter experience and try to stop history from repeating itself. According to writers Mark Fainaru-Wada and Lance Williams, the only way for the healing to begin amid the steroid controversy was for "the game . . . to confront the issue of tainted records. Baseball needed to get to the bottom of the drug use that lay beneath the magical 1998 season of [the record-breaking home run duel between Mark] McGwire and [Sammy] Sosa. It needed to launch a probe into Bonds's 73-homer season."[48]

Continued Clampdown

While that probe remains in limbo, the clampdown on professional athletes goes on. In August 2008 Ukrainian heptathlete Lyudmila Blonska was stripped of a silver medal at the Beijing Olympics for testing positive for the anabolic steroid methyltestosterone. The IOC also considered banning Blonska from the sport for life. British competitor Kelly Sotherton remained incensed: "I'm not happy she competed again. We have rules in our country that we abide by. We don't bring anybody who cheated previously, so why should any other country? I'd have been really upset if she'd won gold. The penalty you should pay if you take drugs is not to compete at the Olympics."[49] The IOC has been at the forefront of antidoping efforts for more than 40 years, and experts say they have been fairly successful in weeding out athletes who use performance-enhancing drugs.

Also, the United States has taken recent steps to curb steroid abuse. George W. Bush signed into law the Anabolic Steroid Control Act of 2004, which requires stiffer penalties for steroid use near sports facilities as well as for those seeking to sell them within 1,000 feet of a sports arena.

Yet even these proactive efforts may not be enough. As recently as 2005, members of a congressional committee looking into allegations of steroid abuse in the National Basketball Association (NBA) mocked the policy already in place, calling it, among other things, "a joke."[50] In questioning NBA officials, including Commissioner David Stern, congressman Tom Davis asked, "How do we know for sure there's no steroid problem in the NBA if its testing policies are so weak?"[51] The NBA and federal government have yet to agree on a stricter policy regarding the use of steroids. Later that same year, congressional officials sought

> " The explosive allegations of steroid use in the late 1990s and early 2000s rocked baseball in much the same way the Sox scandal had. "

tougher standards for nearly all professional sports, much to the annoyance of National Hockey League (NHL) deputy commissioner Bill Daly.

> In August 2008 Ukrainian heptathlete Lyudmila Blonska was stripped of a silver medal at the Beijing Olympics for testing positive for the anabolic steroid methyltestosterone.

"We don't at all agree that the program we have negotiated and implemented is weak," he later wrote. "To the contrary, we believe we have a very strong program in a sport that has no experience or history of problems with performance-enhancing drugs."[52]

Despite Daly's complaining, California representative Henry Waxman reminded athletes and society at large about the ease with which steroids can be purchased. "Dangerous and illegal steroids are just a mouse click away. Parents, teachers, and coaches are on the front lines in the fight against steroid abuse, and they need to know that young athletes and other youth have such easy access to these harmful substances."[53]

Awareness, Waxman implied, was the first step in reducing the popularity of steroids among young athletes. But the congressman also knew that serious and significant efforts are needed to change the perceptions. The truth is steroids work. Only through education, say experts, will the true nature of steroids and their dangers be heard.

The ATLAS Program

While hundreds of antidoping prevention programs claim to help young people avoid the pitfalls of steroid use, it may be another decade before their long-term impact is known. One program, developed by sports medicine specialist Linn Goldberg and internist Diane Elliot, is Athletes Training and Learning to Avoid Steroids (ATLAS). At the moment, young women are one of Goldberg's chief concerns: "In the early 90s, a study showed that 5.6 percent of varsity football players had tried steroids," he says. "Girls nationwide now are almost at the same level as varsity football players were then."[54]

Aside from showing their young charges graphic pictures of overdeveloped bodybuilders, Goldberg and Elliot speak honestly and bluntly about the fact that while steroids no doubt produce results, the health risks outweigh any potential rewards. But Goldberg also knows the reality: The competition for scholarships is stiff, and male and female athletes will often try steroids to give them that extra edge. Goldberg, therefore, stresses an approach that "motivates and empowers student athletes to make the right choices about steroid use."[55]

Research suggests that ATLAS is both effective and cheap. Fifteen schools in Washington and Oregon reported a 50 percent reduction rate of steroid use, as well as a drop in the consumption of alcohol and other drugs. In an ATLAS program in Salt Lake City, Utah, three-fourths of students said they were now less likely to try illegal drugs. As for cost, school districts pay roughly $4 per student. The largest cost ($280) is for the coaches manual.

While there are a host of antidoping programs throughout the United States, ATLAS is one of the first with proven, consistent results. Beyond that, say experts, education about anabolic steroids is everyone's responsibility. And although the number of users may drop, eradication is unlikely: "If it's not steroids it'll be something else that will filter on down," says Frank Uryasz, president of the National Center for Drug Free Sport. "We really have to approach this issue on a broader scale. We need to educate kids on what's right or wrong."[56]

Health teachers and coaches across the country are doing just that, but they cannot be successful, says Jeff Scudder, who teaches at South Broward High School in Florida, without the support of parents: "When you know that your child is willing to take a protein shake and put in those extra hours at the gym, you need to sit down and have a talk. Ask: 'What are your goals? Is someone guiding you to make sure you do this right?' It's not a reason to panic but if they are willing to take shakes, that could blossom into something more."[57]

> George W. Bush signed into law the Anabolic Steroid Control Act of 2004, which requires stiffer penalties for steroid use near sports facilities as well as for those seeking to sell them within 1,000 feet of a sports arena.

Asking Questions, Seeking Answers

Four-time Olympic medal winner Ato Boldon speaks with regret about fellow athletes who use drugs to excel. Although the track and field star's Web site touts that he has been "drug free since 1973," the year of his birth, Boldon says that "I am ashamed, quite frankly, of my generation and what we did. We left the sport kind of tattered."[58]

Former steroid user Chris Bell's opinion on performance-enhancing drugs is more mixed. Hailing from Poughkeepsie, New York, Bell and his two brothers literally grew up on steroids, although they kept their habit a secret from their parents. Bell eventually stopped taking the drugs while his brothers continued. Instead of power-lifting, Bell decided to make a documentary about the culture of steroids. His *Bigger, Stronger, Faster* premiered to critical acclaim at the Sundance Film Festival in 2008, but his three-year journey to make the film did not exactly bring him the definitive answer he might have been looking for. Instead, it only raised more questions.

> While there are a host of antidoping programs throughout the United States, AT-LAS is one of the first with proven, consistent results.

During interviews to promote the movie, Bell spoke of his ambivalence. On one hand, he understood the desire in some to look better and feel stronger. Yet, having decided to quit taking them himself, he worried about the health of his two brothers. Was it worth it, he wondered? How do families talk about such issues? What, if anything, could be done or should be done to curtail steroid use? Bell also wondered how, with so many steroids on the market, is society to decide what is banned and what is not: "I just don't know if I think they should be a controlled substance, the way they are now. If you look at all the laws in our country, and at how and why things get banned, they don't actually fit into that category: They're not addictive, they don't actually kill people. I don't condone the stuff, but after three years of researching this, it seems like we should take another look."[59]

How Can Steroid Use Be Prevented?

66When I got here in 1979, there were some hotbeds of steroid user-abusers in the NFL. After our Super Bowl, a lot of people started taking a new stance. The league began implementing some drug-testing policies. It started to be on the wane.99

—Dan Hampton, quoted in Fred Mitchell, "Butkus Tackles Steroids," *Chicago Tribune,* July 12, 2008, Sports.

Hall of Fame defensive end Dan Hampton now encourages young athletes to avoid taking steroids.

....

66Steroids are dangerous and sometimes fatal. Yet, if some players use them, others will feel the pressure to use them as well, in order to compete.99

—Thomas Sowell, "MLB Steroid Scandal: Say It Ain't So," *Human Events*, December 17, 2007.

Sowell is a senior fellow at the Hoover Institution.

....

* Editor's Note: While the definition of a primary source can be narrowly or broadly defined, for the purposes of Compact Research, a primary source consists of: 1) results of original research presented by an organization or researcher; 2) eyewitness accounts of events, personal experience, or work experience; 3) first-person editorials offering pundits' opinions; 4) government officials presenting political plans and/or policies; 5) representatives of organizations presenting testimony or policy.

66 We've driven this behavior underground and we have all these guys doing it illegally and we don't really know much about it and we need to explore it more. 99

—Chris Bell, interviewed on *Talk of the Nation,* National Public Radio, June 12, 2008.

Bell is a filmmaker and former bodybuilder.

....

66 Steroid scandals will abate as the drugs are reluctantly accepted as inevitable products of a continuing revolution in biotechnology. 99

—Stephen Holden, "Steroid Myth, Scandals and Dreams," *New York Times,* Arts, May 30, 2008.

Holden is a culture critic.

....

66 An athlete properly educated by loving parents, caring coaches, and involved administrators—all of whom aggressively and persistently discourage the use of steroids, deplore other forms of drug abuse, supervise the sketchy world of supplement use, condone good sportsmanship, and encourage the overall pursuit of exemplary citizenship—is an athlete already on the road to success in life, not just competitive sports. 99

—John McCloskey and Julian Bailes, *When Winning Costs Too Much.* Lanham, MD: Taylor Trade, 2005.

McCloskey is a senior editor with the *Houston Chronicle.* Bailes is a professor and neurosurgeon.

....

66 We need to send the right signals to student-athletes. Steroids are unacceptable. Steroids are cheating, and they are banned by our national drug laws.**99**

—U.S. representative Stephen F. Lynch, quoted in Kat Dowling, "Steroid Prevention Efforts Must Start Early, Panel Says," *Daily Free Press,* May 6, 2005. http://media.www.dailyfreepress.com.

Lynch represents the Ninth District of Massachusetts.

66 Individuals who are taking performance enhancing drugs, where does it end? Because you have to look in the mirror every single day and you have to know that you do this on your own.**99**

—Wendy Boglioli, quoted in PBS, "Secrets of the Dead: Doping for Gold," transcript, May 14, 2008. www.pbs.org.

Boglioli won gold and bronze medals in swimming at the 1976 Olympic Games in Montreal, Canada.

66 You get a level playing field only when the fans demand it.**99**

—Bill Moyers, "America on Steroids: A Bill Moyers Essay," *Bill Moyers Journal,* PBS, December 21, 2007. www.pbs.org.

Moyers, a longtime journalist, is the author of many books, including *The Power of Myth.*

How Can Steroid Use Be Prevented?

- The NCAA spends **$4 million** annually on its entire drug testing program.

- Typically, between **1 and 2 percent** of the NCAA tests return with positive traces of banned substances.

- The NCAA tests approximately **13,500** student-athletes for banned substances each year.

- A recent NCAA study reports that **67 percent** of the nearly **21,000** student athletes surveyed believe drug testing is a deterrent for them or their teammates.

- According to Addiction Intervention Resources, simply teaching students about the adverse effects of steroid use is **not enough** to help them avoid trying them.

- High school antisteroid programs can cost as much as **$50,000** per school district.

- President George W. Bush signed the Anabolic Steroid Control Act of 2004, making the **penalties stiffer** for buying and selling steroids.

- In September 2008 defamed gold medalist **Marion Jones** was released from prison after six months. She was jailed for lying in court about her steroid use.

- The NFL currently earmarks **$1.4 million** for the ATLAS and ATHENA anti-steroid programs.

- NFL ATLAS and ATHENA programs educate approximately **36,000 students** per year across the United States.

- Students who participate in the ATLAS and ATHENA programs report **higher self-esteem**, better **self-confidence**, and greater steroid **awareness** after completing the program.

- **Sixty percent** of the ATLAS and ATHENA curriculum is administered by peers.

Fewer High School Seniors Consider Steroids Harmful

The following survey looks at how seniors in high school perceive the potential dangers of steroids. In 1998, 68 percent of seniors believed anabolic steroids were harmful; by 2005, the percentage had dropped to 56. However, more than 50 percent still think steroids are harmful.

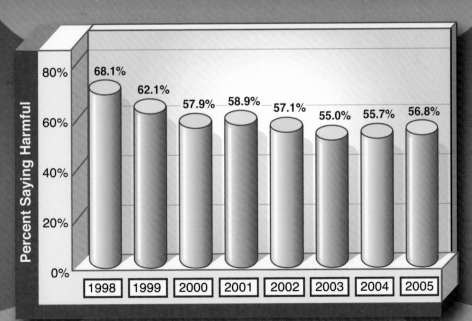

Source: NIDA, "Research Report Series," 2006. www.nida.nih.gov.

Education Can Discourage Steroid Use

Researchers suggest that education is the best way to combat the use of steroids in teenagers. This poster is the kind of tool used in schools and drug prevention programs across the United States to discourage young people from taking steroids.

What are anabolic steroids and what are they used for?

Steroids are synthetic substances that mimic the bodybuilding characteristics of the natural male anabolic hormone testosterone. Steroid use increases muscle mass and strength and may reduce healing time after injury. Without a doctor's prescription, however, steroids are illegal.

What's the big deal?

Besides the risks to the heart, liver, and other organs, steroid use among teens can retard natural growth. Synthetic hormones fool the body into believing it has gone through puberty, thus bones stop growing too soon. So kids get muscles but never get very tall.

What do they look like?

Steroids can be swallowed or injected. Some steroids come in powder form. Not all powder supplements are steroids.

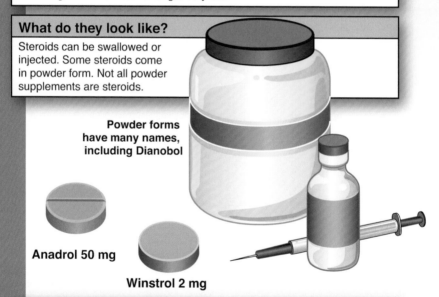

Powder forms have many names, including Dianobol

Anadrol 50 mg

Winstrol 2 mg

Are steroids addictive?

The jury may be out, but evidence points that way. Frequent users may exhibit many of the classic characteristics of addiction, including cravings and withdrawal symptoms.

What to do if you suspect your child is using steroids

Call your family doctor. There is a simple urine test that can be done in the doctor's office. Your child may be having issues with body image, self-esteem or unrealistic athletic ambitions that might require attention from a mental health professional.

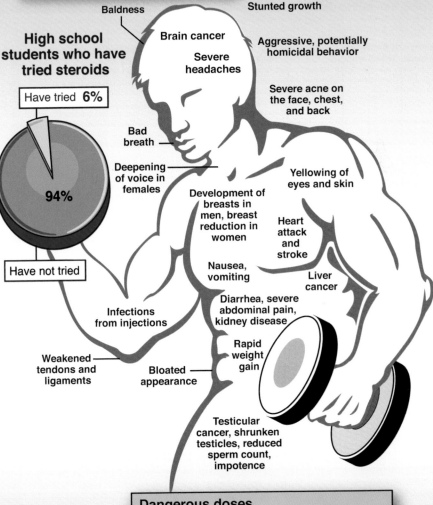

Effects of steroid abuse

Increased muscle mass is only one effect of steroid use. Other effects range from acne to homicidal rampages, also called "roid rage." Users often exhibit one or more of these symptoms.

Severe depression, mood swings, paranoia, anxiety

HIV, hepatitis B, hepatitis C

Sleep problems

Shortened life span

Stunted growth

Baldness

Brain cancer

Severe headaches

Aggressive, potentially homicidal behavior

Severe acne on the face, chest, and back

High school students who have tried steroids

Have tried **6%**

94%

Have not tried

Bad breath

Deepening of voice in females

Development of breasts in men, breast reduction in women

Yellowing of eyes and skin

Heart attack and stroke

Nausea, vomiting

Liver cancer

Infections from injections

Diarrhea, severe abdominal pain, kidney disease

Weakened tendons and ligaments

Bloated appearance

Rapid weight gain

Testicular cancer, shrunken testicles, reduced sperm count, impotence

Dangerous doses

Healthy men may produce less than 10 milligrams of testosterone a day. There are athletes who may use hundreds of milligrams of steroids a day, far exceeding any dose that might be legitimately prescribed by a doctor.

Source: Bill Thornbro, "What You Should Know About Performance-Enhancing Steroids," 2007.

75

High Schools Crack Down

This chart surveys four states—Texas, Florida, New Jersey, and Illinois—and looks at the costs of testing student athletes for steroids, the fees involved, and the penalties for those who test positive for banned substances. Indiana, Missouri, and California are also taking measures to prevent or stop steroid use.

State	Start of testing	Cost per year	Funded by	Who gets tested	Number tested	Penalty for failing
New Jersey	2006–2007 school year	$100,000	State legislation and State Interscholastic Athletics Association; each pay half	Those competing in state championship events	Over 500 in first year, one tested positive	One-year loss of eligibility
Florida	2007–2008 school year	$100,000	State legislation	Football players, baseball players, and weight lifters	One percent of competitors in aforementioned sports	Suspension from team
Texas	February 2008	$3 million	State legislation has set aside money for the program, the most comprehensive – and most expensive – testing program to date	All public high school athletes, both in and out of season	Up to 50,000 students by June 2009	30-day suspension for first violation, calender-year suspension for second, permanent ban from sports for third
Illinois	2008–2009 school year	Estimated $100,000–150,000	Illinois High School Association (no state funding)	Those competing in postseason events	N/A	To be determined

Bills proposed	Early talks	Alternative methods
Indiana	**Missouri**	**California**
A recently proposed bill will initiate testing of 1 percent of high school football and baseball athletes. The testing of 1,600 randomly selected athletes is slated to begin July 1, 2009, at an estimated cost of up to $42,000 from the state.	State Sen. Matt Bartle (R.) met with Kevin Urhahn from the National Center for Drug Free Sport to discuss potential steroid testing programs. In the past, Bartle backed a bill calling for schools to begin steroid testing.	The state has new regulations requiring parents, athletes, and school officials to sign contracts that promise to avoid steroid use. Coaches must also earn certificates in steroid abuse education by this year. All dietary supplements distributed by coaches to athletes must be regulated as well.

Source: *New York Daily News*, "State of the Union: A Look at What Others Have Done," January 31, 2008.

Key People and Advocacy Groups

ATLAS (Athletes Training & Learning to Avoid Steroids): ATLAS is an award-winning, scientifically proven program for male athletes. Its multiple components provide healthy sports nutrition and strength training alternatives to the use of alcohol and illicit and performance-enhancing drugs. ATLAS is peer led and gender specific. It is interactive, engaging, and easy to implement by coaches during the sports season.

Bay Area Laboratory Co-Operative (BALCO): At the center of the steroids storm since 2003, BALCO began by selling food supplements and blood and urine tests to its clients. One of the company's more popular products was tetrahydrogestrinone, also known as "The Clear," a steroid that was initially undetectable.

Chris Bell: A filmmaker and former steroid user, Bell's documentary, *Bigger, Stronger, Faster*, had its world premiere at the 2008 Sundance Film Festival in Park City, Utah.

Barry Bonds: One of the more accomplished and controversial figures in the annals of contemporary sport. In 2001 Bonds broke the single-season home run record (73) and six years later broke Hank Aaron's all-time home run record. Yet Bonds's alleged steroid use has tainted his image and called into question his staggering statistics.

José Canseco: A former outfielder and designated hitter, Canseco was an enthusiastic steroid user for much of his 12-year career. He also "blew the whistle" on a number of his major-league colleagues in his 2005 book *Juiced* and claims that 85 percent of major-league ballplayers took steroids.

Roger Clemens: The winner of 7 Cy Young Awards, Clemens gained a reputation as a fierce competitor during his 24 seasons in the major leagues. But Clemens's reputation took a hit in 2008, when former trainer Brian McNamee testified before a Senate committee that he had injected Clemens with steroids during the 1998, 2000, and 2001 seasons.

Tom Davis: As ranking minority member of the House Committee on Oversight and Government Reform, this Virginia congressman helped organize hearings on steroid use in Major League Baseball.

The Endocrine Society: Founded in 1916, the Endocrine Society is the world's oldest, largest, and most active organization devoted to research on hormones and the clinical practice of endocrinology. The society works to foster a greater understanding of endocrinology among the general public and practitioners of complementary medical disciplines and to promote the interests of all endocrinologists at the national scientific research and health policy levels of government.

Linn Goldberg: For more than two decades Goldberg has been at the forefront of steroids education. He currently heads the Division of Health Promotion and Sports Medicine and is the director of the Human Performance Laboratory at the Oregon Health & Sciences University in Portland.

International Olympic Committee (IOC): The IOC is an international nongovernmental nonprofit organization and the creator of the Olympic Movement. The IOC exists to serve as an umbrella organization of the Olympic Movement. Its primary responsibility is to supervise the organization of the summer and winter Olympic Games.

National Collegiate Athletics Association (NCAA): The NCAA is the primary governing body for the athletic programs of thousands of colleges and universities across the United States.

National Institute on Drug Abuse (NIDA): The National Institute on Drug Abuse is part of the National Institutes of Health, a component of the U.S. Department of Health and Human Services. The institute's mission is to lead the nation in bringing the power of science to bear on drug abuse and addiction.

Bud Selig: Commissioner of Major League Baseball since 1992, Selig has guided "America's Pastime" through years of challenge and of triumph, including the 1994 players' strike, the advent of revenue sharing, and the infamous steroids scandal of the late 1990s.

United States Food and Drug Administration (FDA): An arm of the federal government, the FDA attempts to protect the public safety by regulating and studying the food supply, medical devices, veterinary products, and drugs.

Henry Waxman: Congressman Waxman, a Democrat from California, led the earliest hearings into steroids in professional sports as chairman of the House Oversight and Government Reform Committee.

Chronology

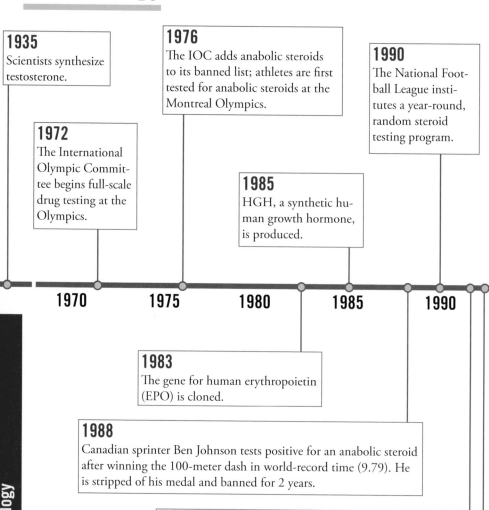

1935
Scientists synthesize testosterone.

1972
The International Olympic Committee begins full-scale drug testing at the Olympics.

1976
The IOC adds anabolic steroids to its banned list; athletes are first tested for anabolic steroids at the Montreal Olympics.

1985
HGH, a synthetic human growth hormone, is produced.

1990
The National Football League institutes a year-round, random steroid testing program.

1970   1975   1980   1985   1990

1983
The gene for human erythropoietin (EPO) is cloned.

1988
Canadian sprinter Ben Johnson tests positive for an anabolic steroid after winning the 100-meter dash in world-record time (9.79). He is stripped of his medal and banned for 2 years.

1992
NFL defensive end Lyle Alzado dies from cancer at age 43. Although unproven, Alzado said his cancer was caused by taking muscle-enhancing drugs.

1993
The Association of Tennis Professionals, the Women's Tennis Association, and the International Tennis Federation create an antidoping program.

2005

Major League Baseball and the National Hockey League institute new policies on steroid use.

In his book *Juiced* slugger José Canseco admits to taking steroids and accuses many MLB stars of using performance-enhancing drugs.

Major leaguers—including Canseco, Rafael Palmeiro, Mark McGwire, and Sammy Sosa—testify before a congressional committee investigating steroid use.

1998

Irish swimmer Michelle Smith, who won three gold medals in the 1996 Olympics, is banned for four years for manipulating a urine sample.

St. Louis Cardinals slugger Mark McGwire admits using the steroid androstenedione.

2000

The World Anti-Doping Agency (WADA) and the U.S. Anti-Doping Agency (USADA) begin operations.

2003

Government agents raid the Bay Area Laboratory Co-Operative (BALCO).

2006

After winning the Tour de France, U.S. cyclist Floyd Landis tests positive for abnormally high levels of testosterone.

2000　2002　2004　2006　2008

2002

As part of a collective bargaining agreement, MLB players and owners agree to hold anonymous testing in 2003. If more than 5 percent are positive, formal testing and penalties will be put into place the next year.

2007

The NFL and its players union announce changes to toughen its steroid policy, including adding EPO to its list of banned substances.

2008

Congress hears testimony involving allegations of steroid use by star pitcher Roger Clemens.

Former Michigan State University football player Tony Mandarich admits taking steroids and cheating on a steroid test in 1988, the year his team won the Rose Bowl.

2004

MLB begins mandatory steroid testing for players; a record 24 athletes are ousted for drug-related violations at the Athens Olympics.

1999

The NBA adds steroids to its list of banned substances.

Related Organizations

Association Against Steroid Abuse

521 N. Sam Houston Pkwy. East, Suite 635

Houston, TX 77060

Web site: www.steroidabuse.com

This association is committed to providing crucial information and statistics on the dangers and issues surrounding anabolic steroid abuse to not only potential abusers, but to parents, educators, sporting organizations, and all others who can help make a difference in this

widespread problem.

Greater Dallas Council on Alcohol and Drug Abuse

4525 Lemmon Ave., Suite 300

Dallas, TX 75219

phone: (214) 522-8600

Web site: www.gdcada.org

The council focuses on reducing the incidence and impact of alcohol and drug use by attracting financial and other support from local, state, and national sources and by implementing quality substance abuse prevention and intervention programs. With the help of the United Way of Metropolitan Dallas, the Texas Department of State Health Services, individuals, corporations, and foundations, the council has grown to annually reach tens of thousands of youth, parents, professionals, and other individuals and groups through an extensive network of supported services.

The Hormone Foundation

8401 Connecticut Ave., Suite 900

Chevy Chase, MD 20815-5817

phone: (800) 467-6663

e-mail: hormone@endo-society.org

Web site: www.hormone.org

The Hormone Foundation, the public education affiliate of the Endocrine Society, is a leading source of hormone-related health information for the public, physicians, allied health professionals, and the media. Its mission is to serve as a resource for the public by promoting the prevention, treatment, and cure of hormone-related conditions through outreach and education.

International Olympic Committee (IOC)

Chateau de Vidy

1007 Lausanne

Switzerland

Web site: www.olympic.org

According to its original charter, the Olympic Movement (and the IOC) contributes to building a peaceful and better world by educating youth through sport practiced without discrimination of any kind and in the Olympic spirit, which requires mutual understanding with a spirit of friendship, solidarity, and fair play.

National Collegiate Athletics Association (NCAA)

700 W. Washington St.

PO Box 6222

Indianapolis, IN 46206-6222

phone: (317) 917-6222

Web site: www.ncaa.org

The NCAA is the primary governing body for the athletic programs of thousands of colleges and universities across the United States. The NCAA has been fighting collegiate drug use for over 30 years and currently spends $4 million a year on its national drug-testing program.

National Federation of State High School Associations (NFHS)

PO Box 690

Indianapolis, IN 46206

phone: (317) 972-6900

Web site: www.nfhs.org

As part of the Make the Right Choice initiative, the NFHS has produced two videos on the dangers of steroid use that can be watched
online.

National Institute on Drug Abuse (NIDA)
National Institutes of Health

6001 Executive Blvd., Room 5213

Bethesda, MD 20892-9561

phone: (301) 443-1124

e-mail: information@nida.nih.gov

Web site: www.nida.nih.gov

As part of the National Institutes of Health, NIDA's mission is to lead
the nation in bringing the power of science to bear on drug abuse and
addiction.

Office of National Drug Control Policy (ONDCP)

Drug Policy Information Clearinghouse

PO Box 6000

Rockville, MD 20849-6000

phone: (800) 666–3332

fax: (301) 519–5212

The principal purpose of ONDCP is to establish policies, priorities, and
objectives for the nation's drug control program. The goals of the program are to reduce illicit drug use, manufacturing, and trafficking; drug-
related crime and violence; and drug-related health consequences.

United States Food and Drug Administration

5600 Fishers Ln.

Rockville, MD 20857

phone: (800) 216-7331

Web site: www.fda.gov

The FDA is responsible for protecting the public health by assuring the safety, efficacy, and security of human and veterinary drugs, biological products, medical devices, the nation's food supply, cosmetics, and products that emit radiation. The FDA is also responsible for advancing the public health by helping to speed innovations that make medicines and foods more effective, safer, and more affordable and by helping the public get the accurate, science-based information they need to use medicines and foods to improve their health.

United States Olympic Committee

Olympic University

1 Olympic Plaza

Colorado Springs, CO 80909

phone: (719) 866-4837

e-mail: olympicuniversity@usoc.org

Web site: http://teamusa.org

The USOC is recognized by the International Olympic Committee as the sole entity in the United States whose mission involves training, entering, and underwriting the full expenses for the U.S. teams in the Olympic, Paralympics, Pan American, and Parapan American Games. The U.S. Olympic Committee also oversees the process by which U.S. cities seek to be selected as a Candidate City to host the Olympic and Paralympics Games, winter or summer, or the Pan American Games.

WebMD

Web site: www.webmd.com

WebMD provides valuable health information, tools for managing health, and support to those who seek information. The WebMD staff blends award-winning expertise in medicine, journalism, health communications, and content creation to provide the best health information possible.

For Further Research

Books

Michael S. Bahrke and Charles E. Yesalis, *Performance-Enhancing Substances in Sport and Exercise*. Champaign, IL: Human Kinetics, 2002.

Howard Bryant, *Juicing the Game*. New York: Viking, 2005.

José Canseco, *Juiced*. New York: Regan, 2005.

Mark Fainaru-Wada and Lance Williams, *Game of Shadows: Barry Bonds, BALCO, and the Steroids Scandal That Rocked Professional Sports*. New York: Gotham, 2006.

Nathan Jendrick, *Dunks, Doubles, Doping*. Guilford, CT: Lyons, 2006.

John McCloskey and Julian Bailes, *When Winning Costs Too Much*. Lanham, MD: Taylor Trade, 2005.

David R. Mottram, *Drugs in Sport*. London: Taylor and Francis, 2005.

Jason Porterfield, *Doping*. New York: Rosen, 2007.

William N. Taylor, *Anabolic Steroids and the Athlete*. Jefferson, NC: McFarland, 2002.

Periodicals

Roger Angell, "Green," *New Yorker*, April 7, 2008.

Tim Christie, "To Catch a Cheat," *Eugene (OR) Register-Guard*, June 29, 2008.

Jeré Longman, "Russian Olympians Suspended for Doping Violations," *New York Times*, August 1, 2008. www.nytimes.com.

Fred Mitchell, "Butkus Tackles Steroids: Former Bear Urges Preps to Believe It's 'Cool to Play Clean,'" *Chicago Tribune*, July 12, 2008.

Thomas Sowell, "MLB Steroid Scandal: Say It Ain't So," *Human Events*, December 17, 2007.

Ryan Young, "Olympic Qualifier Jaben Tests Positive for Steroids: Trip to Beijing in Doubt," *Kansas City (MO) Star*, July 18, 2008.

Internet Sources

Luke Andrews, "Steroid Prevention the NCAA Way," CBS Sports, June 9, 2006. www.cstv.com/sports/m-footbl/uwire/060906aab.html.

Mike Celizic, "Time for Steroid Testing in High School," NBC Sports, April 24, 2004. www.msnbc.msn.com/id/4556250.

Bryan Curtis, "The Juice and I: Jose Canseco and Steroids, a Love Story," *Slate*, February 18, 2005. www.slate.com/id/2113745.

Edward Epstein, "Schwarzenegger Linked to Contests with Steroids," *San Francisco Chronicle*, October 1, 2003. www.sfgate.com/cgi-bin/article.cgi?f=/c/a/2003/10/01/MN191094.DTL.

National Public Radio, "Are Steroids as 'American as Apple Pie?'" *Talk of the Nation*, June 12, 2008. www.npr.org/templates/story/story.php?storyId=91432799.

PBS, "Secrets of the Dead: Doping for Gold," May 14, 2008. www.pbs.org/wnet/secrets/transcripts/doping-for-gold-program-transcript.

USA Today, "Drugs in Sports: Linn Goldberg," December 8, 2004. http://cgi1.usatoday.com/mchat/20041208004/tscript.htm.

Source Notes

Overview

1. José Canseco, *Juiced*. New York: HarperCollins, 2005, p. 3.
2. Quoted in isteroids blog, "Steroids Work," August 2008. www.isteroids.com.
3. Quoted in *USA Today*, "Drugs in Sports: Linn Goldberg," December 8, 2004. http://cgi1.usatoday.com.
4. Quoted in Cate Baily, "Behind the Bulk: Craig's Story," *Anabolic Steroids*, NIDA for Teens: The Science Behind Drug Abuse, 2003. http://teens.drugabuse.gov.
5. Quoted in Drugstory.org, "Sports, Steroids, and Teens." www.drugstory.org.
6. Quoted in *ESPN: Track and Field*, "Report: Jones Used Steroids for Two Years Before 2000 Games," October 5, 2007. http://sports.espn.go.com.
7. John McCloskey and Julian Bailes, *When Winning Costs Too Much*. Lanham, MD: Taylor Trade, 2005, p. 67.
8. McCloskey and Bailes, *When Winning Costs Too Much*, p. 67.
9. Quoted in *USA Today*, "Drugs in Sports: Linn Goldberg."
10. Quoted in Gregg Jones and Gary Jacobson, "The Secret Edge: Steroids in High Schools," *Dallas Morning News*, 2005. www.dallasnews.com.
11. Quoted in MLB.com, "Opening Statement of Brian Gerald McNamee," February 13, 2008. http://mlb.mlb.com.
12. Quoted in CBS News, "Clemens Vehemently Denies Steroid Use," *60 Minutes*, January 6, 2008. www.cbsnews.com.
13. Quoted in Ray Hall, "World's Fastest Female Had Guilty Secret," *Louisville Courier-Journal*, October 25, 2007, p. 4C.
14. Quoted in ESPN, "Mitchell Report: Baseball Slow to React to Players' Steroid Use," December 1, 2007. http://sports.espn.go.com.
15. Quoted in A.J. Perez, "NFL Earmarks $1.4 million for Serious Anti-steroid Message to Youths," *USA Today*, August 31, 2008. www.usatoday.com.

How Serious a Problem Is Steroid Use?

16. Quoted in Jones and Jacobson, "The Secret Edge."
17. Quoted in Jacobson and Jones, "The Secret Edge."
18. Quoted in Jacobson and Jones, "The Secret Edge."
19. Quoted in Jacqueline Stenson, "Kids on Steroids Willing to Risk It All for Success," MSNBC, March 3, 2008. www.msnbc.msn.com.
20. Quoted in Sheryl Ubelacker, "Typical Steroid User Not Elite Athlete but Regular Guy Seeking Buff Body: Study," AOL Health, October 11, 2007. http://aol.mediresource.com.
21. Quoted in *Science Daily*, "The 'Arms' Race: Adult Steroid Users Seek Muscles, Not Medals," October 12, 2007. www.sciencedaily.com.
22. Carol Emery Normandi and Laurelee Roark, *It's Not About Food*. New York: Perigee, 1999, p. xx.
23. Quoted in Ellen Mitchell, "Bodybuilders Resist Laws Against Steroids," *New York Times*, April 26, 1992. http://query.nytimes.com.
24. Quoted in McCloskey and Bailes, *When Winning Costs Too Much*, p. 131.
25. Quoted in McCloskey and Bailes, *When Winning Costs Too Much*, p. 131.

26. Quoted in Jay Paris, "Steroids: Dangerous, Illegal and So Very Easy to Obtain," *San Diego North County Times*, April 16, 2005. www.nctimes.com.

27. Quoted in United Press International, "Easy for Youth to Get Anabolic Steroids," July 21, 2008. www.upi.com.

28. Quoted in A.J. Perez, "Study Finds Steroids, Illegal Stimulants in Supplements," *USA Today*, December 5, 2007. www.usatoday.com.

How Dangerous Are Steroids?

29. Adam Conn, "Confessions of a Steroid User," Contractbud.com, May 1, 2005. http://contractbud.com.

30. Quoted in BBC News, "Bodybuilder Scarred from Steroids," August 21, 2008. http://news.bbc.co.uk.

31. Quoted in Melissa Dahl, "Steroid Abuse Scars a Young Muscle Man for Life," MSNBC, August 26, 2008. http://bodyodd.msnbc.msn.com.

32. Quoted in Michael S. Schmidt, "Steroid Maker Says He Taught About N.F.L. Loopholes," *New York Times*, May 2, 2008. www.nytimes.com.

33. Quoted in Jeré Longman, "East German Steroids' Toll: 'They Killed Heidi,'" *New York Times*, January 26, 2004. www.nytimes.com.

34. Quoted in Longman, "East German Steroids' Toll."

35. Quoted in Stan Grossfeld, "A Sad and Revealing Tale of Steroid Use," *Boston Globe/International Herald Tribune*, February 20, 2008. www.iht.com.

36. Quoted in Grossfeld, "A Sad and Revealing Tale of Steroid Use."

37. Craig Davidson, "From Mr. Average . . . to Superman," *Guardian*, May 18, 2008. www.guardian.co.uk.

38. Quoted in CNN, "'Roid Rage' Questions Surround Benoit Murder-Suicide," June 29, 2007. www.cnn.com.

39. Quoted in The Story, American Public Media, "Roid Rage," April 4, 2007. http://thestory.org.

40. Lyle Alzado, as told to Shelley Smith, "I'm Sick and I'm Scared," *Sports Illustrated*, July 8, 1991, p. 21.

Should Steroid Testing and Laws Be Strengthened?

41. Quoted in Tim Marchman, "Steroid Sting Is Mere Tip of the Iceberg," *New York Sun*, September 25, 2007. www.nysun.com.

42. Mark Fainaru-Wada and Lance Williams, *Game of Shadows: Barry Bonds, BALCO, and the Steroids Scandal That Rocked Professional Sports*. New York: Gotham, 2006, p. 57.

43. Quoted in Jeré Longman, "Russian Olympians Suspended for Doping Violations," *New York Times*, August 1, 2008. www.nytimes.com.

44. Quoted in ESPN/Associated Press, "Lowell Calls for Future Steroid Tests to Be 100 Percent Accurate in Recent Speech," January 18, 2008. http://sports.espn.go.com.

45. Quoted in Dan Connolly, "Suspensions, Not Fines, to Be Steroid Test Penalty," *Baltimore Sun*, March 21, 2005. www.baltimoresun.com.

46. Quoted in Juliet Macur, "Landis Loses His Case and Title," *New York Times*, September 21, 2007, p. 1.

47. Quoted in Kate Ravilious, "Barry Bonds Steroid Debate Highlights History of Drugs in Sports," *National Geographic News*, June 22, 2007. http://news.nationalgeographic.com.

How Can Steroid Abuse Be Prevented?

48. Fainaru-Wada and Williams, *Game of Shadows*, p. 264.

49. Quoted in *Daily Telegraph* (UK), "Ukraine Athlete Lyudmila Blonska Stripped

of Heptathlon Silver Medal for Doping," August 22, 2008. www.telegraph.co.uk.

50. Quoted in ESPN, "Reform Committee Drafting Testing Law for Major Sports," May 19, 2005. http://sports.espn.go.com.

51. Quoted in ESPN, "Reform Committee Drafting Testing Law for Major Sports."

52. Quoted in Fox News, "Congress Eyes NFL, NBA, NHL Steroids Stance," November 17, 2005. www.foxnews.com.

53. Quoted in Elizabeth White, "Congress: Getting Steroids Easy," BG News, November 2, 2005. http://media.www.bgnews.com.

54. Quoted in Bonnie DiSimone, "Schools' Prevention Efforts Aim to Halt Rise of Steroid Use," *New York Times*, June 5, 2005. www.nytimes.com.

55. Quoted in Robert Mathias, "Steroid Prevention Program Scores with High School Athletes," *NIDA Notes*, July/August, 1997. www.nida.nih.gov.

56. Quoted in McCloskey and Bailes, *When Winning Costs Too Much*, p. 117.

57. Quoted in McCloskey and Bailes, *When Winning Costs Too Much*, p. 122.

58. Ato Boldon, quoted on Ato Boldon Web site. http://atoboldon.com.

59. Quoted in Bilge Ebiri, "Filmmaker Christopher Bell on *Bigger, Stronger, Faster*, Steroids, and How to Cheat at the Olympics," *New York Magazine*, May, 28, 2008. http://nymag.com.

List of Illustrations

Index

Index

About the Author

David Robson is the recipient of a National Endowment for the Arts grant and two playwriting fellowships from the Delaware Division of the Arts. His dramatic work has been performed across the country. David is also the author of many books for young adults on subjects ranging from the John F. Kennedy assassination to the Black Arts Movement. David lives with his wife and daughter in Wilmington, Delaware.